Understanding
Bible Prophecy

Morris A. Inch

Understanding
Bible Prophecy

HARPER & ROW, PUBLISHERS
NEW YORK, HAGERSTOWN, SAN FRANCISCO, LONDON

UNDERSTANDING BIBLE PROPHECY. Copyright © 1977 by Morris A. Inch.
All rights reserved. Printed in the United States of America. No part of
this book may be used or reproduced in any manner whatsoever without
written permission except in the case of brief quotations embodied in
critical articles and reviews: For information address Harper & Row,
Publishers, Inc., 10 East 53rd Street, New York, N.Y. 10022. Published
simultaneously in Canada by Fitzhenry & Whiteside Limited, Toronto.

FIRST EDITION

Designed by Stephanie Krasnow

Library of Congress Cataloging in Publication Data

Inch, Morris A
    Understanding Bible prophecy.
    1. Bible—Prophecies. I. Title.
BS647.2.I5 1977   220.1'5   77–2608
ISBN 0-06-064087-1 pbk.

---

77 78 79 80 10 9 8 7 6 5 4 3 2 1

Contents

Preface

This book is directed toward those interested in prophecy or turned off by what so often disguises itself as prophecy. It attempts a systematic treatment, without recourse to textbook quotations, technical vocabulary, or labored argument.

I rely on extensive biblical and personal illustrations—the former to introduce prophetic literature and the latter to clarify a point. The combination is intended to encourage the reader to consider the topic further.

The contents page, providing chapter titles and brief resumés, suggests the ground that is covered. There are seven areas in all, some divided not only for discussion's sake but also to make helpful divisions for study groups to manage in a yearly quarter. I hope this will be a useful guide for individual or group inquiry. Scripture is quoted from the New American Standard Bible.

I am indebted to those instructors who urged upon me the importance of a balanced approach to any subject, and I would like to offer a special word of appreciation to Gary Arnold for his assistance.

I

Nature of Prophecy

Prophecy is not simply foretelling, as commonly assumed, but forthtelling. What do you think about when the subject of prophecy is mentioned? A gypsy fortuneteller, bent over her crystal ball, peering into the future? An elaborate wall chart, marked in contrasting colors, detailing events of the last times? These images mislead us into thinking prophecy is primarily concerned with revealing future events.

Who comes to mind as a prophet? Michel Nostradamus, that surprising seer of an earlier generation? The contemporary Jeane Dixon? These figures confuse our thinking about prophecy because they predict the future.

Prophecy is forthtelling or disclosing. The prophet said it was "the word of the Lord" (Joel 1:1), God's admonition to man.

> "Yet even now," declares the Lord,
> "Return to Me with all your heart,
> And with fasting, weeping, and mourning" (Joel 2:12).

Captivity loomed before the Hebrew people, "for the Lord . . . [had] spoken" (Joel 3:8). The prophetic theme runs throughout the Book of Joel, setting before the people what God would have them know and act upon. The same is true of Isaiah, Jeremiah, Hosea, Micah, and the other prophetic writings; the pattern never varies. "Thus says the Lord" marks the prophet's message. He is never asked to foretell but to "tell forth" the word of the Lord. Prophecy is nothing more or less than God's disclosure. In order to become accustomed to thinking of prophecy in this manner, we can cultivate the attitude expressed by young Samuel: "Speak, for Thy servant is listening" (1 Sam. 3:10).

Chaos of the Cults

One leisurely afternoon I was disturbed by a gentle rapping at my door. I reluctantly made my way to answer the summons and was confronted by a disarmingly attractive girl, whose appearance at first distracted my attention from her explanation of the purpose of her visit. She was, by her happy insight, one of God's chosen. She alleged to have all pertinent truth concerning the last days.

We talked a few moments, and she seemed doubtful that I could actually be acquainted with the teaching of the Jehovah's Witnesses and still question its accuracy. She was not well versed in the doctrine herself and may have been a rather recent convert or a second-generation adherent. Whatever the case, she did not seem overly zealous. Although she clearly felt frustrated by her inability to transmit her faith, she was unable to accept any alternate interpretation of biblical teaching. So she took an abrupt leave, as if she could thereby demonstrate her faithfulness to the Commission and my unwillingness to respond.

What was God's word for me in light of this girl's claim upon truth? Quickly, urgently, the question burned into my thinking, the alternative being a one-way ticket to the Brooklyn headquarters of the Jehovah's Witnesses. I could almost see my uncritical scalp hanging in their trophy room, one more statistic in their meticulous accounting system.

On another occasion, two young men proceeded with a much more subtle assault in introducing their scheme for understanding life. Seeing that I was sitting alone with my thoughts, they took seats beside me, commenting on the need of faith for such times as these. They acknowledged that Jesus had spoken to his time and promised another to replace him, a promise they judged fulfilled by Baha'ullah. This was but one of numerous contacts I have had with persons of the Bahai faith and their easy syncretism, which erodes the centrality of Christ.

Once again I was driven to consider God's revelation. Were it not for a good deal of deliberate reflection on the prophetic message, I should likely be warming my feet at a Bahai fireside.

The babble of the cults, swelling on every side, accents the importance of our quest for a true understanding of prophecy. William James argued that some questions are so trivial we need not concern ourselves with them. No doubt that is true, but the inquiry into prophecy touches the pulse of life itself. It struggles with our significance as persons and works where a blunder may prove critical.

The Year of Marx

For an increasing percentage of the world this is not anno Domini but the year of Karl Marx. His ideology, less than a century and a half old, has extended its grasp to an astonishingly large following.

Marx was of Jewish descent and converted to Protestantism out of what seems to have been prudential considerations, before reaching the conclusion that "man makes religion, religion does not make man." Marx saw a new world in the offing, without a place for God.

A visitor had been sharing his Christian faith with African hosts when he overheard one of them whisper to a friend concerning the claims made by communism. His host shrugged and said, "Who can say which of them is correct?" We had better know what we believe and why we believe it before stepping out into today's world, that is, if we want a sympathetic hearing.

Three types of Communists come to mind. One resembles the stereotyped world revolutionary who would likely turn his own mother in to the authorities if she strayed from the party line. He keeps his ears open for any possible implications in what his associates say in passing and is ready to snuff out incipient heresy before it can take root. The second plays a live-and-let-live role. He could easily adjust to a non-Communist situation as long as there were enough creature comforts and especially a young lady to meet his fancy. The third is the most attractive individual so far as his outlook on life is concerned. He manifests a crusading spirit for his cause, along with a deep concern for human values. He could read 1 Corinthians 13 and assimilate it as his own, out of context to be sure, but adapted to his frame of reference.

These three types illustrate the diversity in communism today. They help us understand why Christians living behind the Iron Curtain talk more often of Communists than communism. They also press home the importance of considering the prophetic message for our time. What does God have to say to us in a period of history that many date with the rise of Karl Marx?

The religious cults greet us on the one side, the antireligious Marxists on the other, and those answers we have prepared and memorized often seem ineffectual when we try to apply them in real-life situations. Like many clichés, our answers are designed to counter a stereotypic attack, but they lose their punch when we try to use them in our debates with real adherents of these religious and secular positions. The words seem to choke in our throats, and we turn to God once more; we appeal to his Word to come to our aid.

Cultural Revival

Western colonialism is receding, and the lands formerly controlled by imperialists are experiencing political and cultural renewal. This may be the most critical development of our time, and it is especially pressing for the Christian faith, which often rode in on the imperialists' coattails and which some think should exit in the same manner.

A certain Jordanian Arab served with the English military under British rule. At one time he seriously considered becoming a Christian; it seemed a rather natural appendix to English occupation and his own cooperation. With the rise of Zionism and the eventual emergence of the Jewish state, he shook off the possibilities he had entertained in the past. He now reaffirms his Moslem commitment and takes an aggressive stand for the Arab cause.

Prooftexting Israel's unqualified right to the land of Palestine seems to him little short of blasphemy. "What an incredible way to use Scripture," he'll gasp, shaking his head less in disbelief than anger. Prediction can, unless it has good biblical ballast, be tossed about like a stick on the waves of cultural revival.

Several Africans argue whether or not to submit their children to the tribal practice of circumcision. "It has pagan roots," warns one.

"Not necessarily," cautions another.

"Not at all in our case," claims a third.

All three face the task of adhering to the faith through a time when the revival of former ways has reached overwhelming proportions. They must think in terms of growing opposition, persecution, even martyrdom, not to mention their own ideals, which are increasingly divorced from those of the foreign missionary.

This may not be the world we would have chosen, but it is

the world that has come about. We can respond too little if we ignore the full counsel of Scripture; we can respond too late if we fail to see how the world threatens to be swept beyond our reach.

The Task

God means to say something to us in light of the developments of our day, but what he says cannot be contrary to what he has previously disclosed. A unity flows throughout although it results in diverse application. Some try to carry Scripture over in a legalistic fashion, perhaps with the best of intentions but with equally disastrous results. They argue as if there were no differences between biblical times and our own and do not seem to appreciate the cultural context in which the revelation is given.

Scripture requires "eye for eye, tooth for tooth, hand for hand, foot for foot, burn for burn, wound for wound, bruise for bruise" (Exod. 21:24–25). A clear enough statement, someone concludes, quite apart from its original context. Or is it?

One particularly dismal day in my childhood my brother, several years older than I, wanted to duel with swords (two sticks selected for the purpose). I was reluctant, believing I would get the worst of the encounter. But he urged me, offering the longer of the two weapons as an inducement. Still hesitant, I agreed and quickly succeeded in thrusting my makeshift sword into his eye. It was a while before we knew if some permanent damage had been done, and I felt terribly guilty over the whole matter. I did not, however, imagine that my parents would retaliate in kind.

Were my parents remiss in their duty? No, their common sense served them well, but they would have been hard put to come up with the reason Scripture should not have been interpreted so as to inflict me with a similar wound.

The biblical injunction, taken in its cultural context, had to do with disproportionate and cruel punishment. Among the tribes and nations surrounding the children of Israel, the smallest infraction could be rewarded with sadistic torture. God prohibited the Hebrew from indulging in such a practice by allowing only punishment equal in kind to the offense.

The prophetic message speaks most pointedly to those who first hear it in their cultural setting, and only indirectly does it apply to anyone else. For example, Jonah, the reluctant prophet, eventually agreed to bring the Almighty's warning of destruction to the great city of Nineveh. God evaluated the inhabitants of that ancient metropolis who could not distinguish "between their right and left hand." Upon hearing the words of the prophet, the city repented, and the Almighty spared them the impending holocaust.

But what does that have to do with Chicago, Detroit, or New York City? Nothing directly, much indirectly. It suggests that God does not sleep through our wickedness and that our sins pile up against us. It also warns us to repent of our evil and turn to God, and it reveals that the Almighty would prefer to forgive us rather than rain down fire from heaven. At this point, however, any similarity between Nineveh and a modern-day city is conjecture. We may draw rough analogies between Chicago and Nineveh, but they would never hold up as conclusive evidence. For example, the precedent of Jonah does not give one the right to purchase a sound truck and broadcast through the streets, "Yet forty days and Chicago will be overthrown."

Nor can we gauge how culpable Chicago has become. "The men of Nineveh shall stand up with this generation at the judgment, and shall condemn it," Jesus warned, "because they repented at the preaching of Jonah; and behold, something greater than Jonah is here (Matt. 12:41). The principle operating here is that "from everyone who has been given much shall much be required; and to whom they entrusted much, of him they will ask all the more" (Luke 12:48). God's Word faith-fully represented heaps condemnation upon those unwilling to act upon the opportunity it affords. Given Chicago's legacy, even the good it sows may appear to God as astonishing neglect. We simply do not know and must leave the judgment with Someone better qualified.

To pick up the number *forty* as the duration for Chicago's respite would be silly. Chances are, the span would run its course, and we would be left trying to figure out a plausible explanation for business as usual on the forty-first day. We would find ourselves scratching our heads to come up with what would pass for a good excuse for a bad projection, attempting to fill in a hole we should never have excavated in the first place.

We should be concerned about *dynamic* rather than *formal* equivalents. Our task is to perceive how Scripture ties into life today. A significant force to be reckoned with or ignored at our own risk, Scripture is always culturally relevant. However, this dynamic/formal distinction must be recognized. For instance, in the New Testament we find the first church members "were taking their meals together" (Acts 2:46). Formal equivalency would require that we also take our food in common no matter how impractical that might be. To do less, the reasoning goes, would be to depreciate Scripture.

The *dynamic* equivalent respects first the historical conditions that encouraged the practice for that time and in those particu-lar circumstances. It may discover differences between the church at Jerusalem and Corinth and certainly between Jerusa-lem and Chicago. It does not hesitate to inquire into what would be an appropriate expression of Christian concern in the latter setting, whether that be reviving the love feast, financing a home for the elderly, providing childcare for working mothers, or any number of equally communal enterprises.

Prophecy is the declaration of God's word. It inevitably

touches on the contemporary situation but by way of the biblical context. God would speak today as his servants listen breathlessly, having pressed beyond prophecy as simple prediction to understanding it as the disclosure of God to man.

Questions for Study and Discussion

1. Why is prophecy a topic of prime importance? Why has its significance been obscured from time to time?

2. Can you think of other current events or movements that could be interpreted more satisfactorily in light of a better understanding of biblical prophecy?

3. What is the major misconception concerning biblical prophecy? Why does it persist?

4. Reflect on the statement that what God "says today cannot be contrary to what he has previously disclosed." What implications does this have for how we interpret Scripture? What limits does it set on understanding prophecy?

5. Distinguish between *dynamic* and *formal* applications of biblical teaching. Can you illustrate them both with practical examples?

6. A *literal* interpretation of the Bible has become a theological battle cry for many. What important concern underlies this expression? On the other hand, how may it be used as an excuse to misappropriate Scripture?

II

Nature of Prophecy [2]

We have stripped away the idea of prophecy as simple prediction and have begun to develop its character as the revelation of God. This shift between perspectives will become more evident as we consider the biblical record.

"Prepare to meet your God, O Israel," thundered Amos (Amos 4:12). The heart of the prophet's concern was a religious message, not primarily emphasizing *what* might come to pass but *who* cradles life in his hands. God is *the* subject of the prophetic message.

Isaiah took up the identical refrain:

> Listen, O heavens, and hear, O earth;
> For the Lord speaks:
> "Sons I have reared and brought up,
> But they have revolted against Me.
> "An ox knows its owner,
> And a donkey its master's manger,
> *But* Israel does not know,
> My people do not understand" (Isa. 1:2–3).

The prophet's burden was that the people might recognize their God; he wanted to see the prodigals come home.

Jeremiah's thrust was even more pointed:

> Thus says the Lord,
> "What injustice did your fathers find in Me,
> That they went far from Me
> And walked after emptiness and became empty" (Jer. 2:5)?

As their fathers had done, the people continued in their wayward direction, giving no thought to the emptiness of their lives or the blessing they were missing.

The prophetic warning that they prepare to meet their God often failed to distract the people from some inclination which seemed more inviting or less demanding. The prophetic message continues to struggle with old adversaries as well as additional opposition.

Old Tensions Revived

Without exception, the nations of the ancient world were religious. The universe often seemed more populated with gods than with men. One awoke with a dim recollection of how the gods had flirted with one's dreams, to face a day in which ritual must be observed in order not to offend some finicky deity. Then came the terrors of another evening since the spirits often chose that time to wander about.

Theistic arguments for the existence of God would have seemed the height of folly in such a setting. Why try to convince people of what they already *knew* to be true? Irreligion appeared more as insanity than impiety; so the prophets were not needed to recall man to religion but rather to the living God. "Repent and turn away from your idols," Ezekiel was coached to say, "and turn your faces away from all your abominations" (Ezek. 14:6). Turn from your images to the Creator, from what he abhors to what pleases him.

One form of this idolatry was astrology, now experiencing an impressive revival. It is generally thought that astrology originated with the Chaldeans prior to 3000 B.C. Observing the relationship of heavenly bodies to our seasons, they concluded that some supernatural force could influence the fate of men and nations. Eventually they develop an elaborate system by which the temperament and destiny of individuals might be determined by the sign of the zodiac under which they were born and by the continuing conjunctions and oppositions of the celestial aggregate.

The prophet's attitude can be gathered from Isaiah's scathing judgment on Babylon in which he lumped sorcerers and astrologers together as vain deliverers of the nation.

> Let now the astrologers,
> Those who prophesy by the stars,
> Those who predict by the new moons,
> Stand up and save you from what will come upon you.
> Behold, they have become like stubble,
> Fire burns them;
> They cannot deliver themselves from the power of the flame;
> There will be no coal to warm by,
> *Nor* a fire to sit before! (Isa. 47:13–14).

This is not the kind of imagery one easily forgets: Sorcerer and astrologer are consumed, leaving no comfort for those circling the now-dead embers.

The Book of Daniel likewise contrasts the prophetic ministry with that of the astrologers (Dan. 1:20, 2:27, 4:7, 5:7). When the latter were unable to interpret the inscription on Belshazzar's wall, Daniel was summoned. "Just now the wise men *and* the conjurers were brought in before me that they might read this inscription and make its interpretation known to me, but they could not declare the interpretation of the message," Belshazzar complained, adding, "but I personally have heard about you, that you are able to give interpretations and solve difficult problems. Now if you are able to read the inscription and make its interpretation known to me, you will be clothed with purple and *wear* a necklace of gold around your neck, and you will have authority as the third *ruler* in the kingdom."

"Keep your gifts for yourself, or give your rewards to someone else," Daniel replied, "however, I will read the inscription to the king and make the interpretation known to him." Thus the prophet began with a reference to "the Most High God" who "granted sovereignty, grandeur, glory, and majesty to Nebuchadnezzar your father," only to punish him for his pride, as he intends to do with Belshazzar as well (see Dan. 5:15–18). Here again is the familiar distinction between prophecy as simple prediction and as revealing the person of God, between astrologer and Hebrew prophet.

What is the significance of the statistic that over 70 percent of the daily newspapers in the United States carry astrological columns? Obviously, it indicates an interest in prediction, but perhaps it also suggests a dearth of understanding or acceptance of the biblical attack on prophecy.

Another competitor of the prophets which has enjoyed a good deal of attention is spiritualism. The best-known biblical example is Saul's visit to the medium of En-dor (1 Sam. 28). Since the Philistines were waging war against him and since God no longer addressed him through "prophets or by dreams," Saul turned to the spiritualist to summon Samuel back from the dead. "Why then do you ask me," Samuel wanted to know, "since the Lord has departed from you and has become your adversary?" The interchange takes on added significance because the medium was prohibited under penalty of death from practicing her trade.

One wonders about professing believers who dutifully attend their home church for the morning service and skip away for an afternoon or evening session with a spiritualist. This practice suggests at the very least a failure to come to grips with the prophetic stance.

We can all profit from listening to Micah's still timely words:

> "I will cut off sorceries from your hand,
> And you will have fortune tellers no more.
> "I will cut off your carved images
> And your sacred pillars from among you,
> So that you will no longer bow down
> To the work of your hands" (Mic. 5:12–13).

Here Micah makes explicit the prophet's belief that occult activity and idolatry are allied against the prophetic message.

Another practice which began in ancient times and persists today is assuming the activity of patron deities. Jeremiah announced God's intent: "I shall make an end of Moab, the one who offers *sacrifice* on the high place and the one who burns incense to his gods" (Jer. 48:35). Their gods will not take the field of battle as the Almighty inflicts those left defenseless.

The Hebrews in that day, no less than we today, could be carried away by misplaced patriotism. "Yet I sent you all My servants the prophets, again and again, saying, 'Oh, do not do this abominable thing which I hate,'" God laments over the Israelites living in Egypt, "but they did not listen or incline their ears to turn from their wickedness, so as not to burn sacrifices to other gods" (Jer. 44:4–5). Taking up the custom of those about them, they cast their lot with the local pantheon.

Partisan idolatry creeps in whenever we make a privileged appeal for our country, when we except it from the obligation to function as a responsible member of the commonwealth of nations, or when we twist its government against the welfare of the people. We sense it at work in the international setting when undue emphasis is laid on national security, as Isaiah faults his associates:

> Woe to those who go down to Egypt for help,
> *And* rely on horses,
> And trust in chariots because they are many,
> And in horsemen because they are very strong,

> But they do not look at the Holy One of Israel, nor seek the
> Lord! (Isa. 31:1).

Rather than assuming the *risk* natural to an interplay of peoples
and seeking justice in their actions, Israel spent herself on building extensive alliances; so Isaiah continued his instruction:

> Now the Egyptians are men, and not God,
> And their horses are flesh and not spirit;
> So the Lord will stretch out His hand,
> And he who helps will stumble
> And he who is helped will fall,
> And all of them will come to an end together (Isa. 31:3).

The prophet portrayed the obsession with national security as
an idolatrous exercise.

It hardly seems necessary to add that the prophet never rejected the legitimacy of national security as such or the role of
the military and alliances per se except when such concerns
assumed the place of the Almighty. It is in fact the responsibility of government to provide order and safety, and government
would be amiss if it did not do so. But its obligation must be
carried out with restraint, and care must be taken that patron
deities not be raised to challenge the sovereign rule of God.

The problem may also become internalized to the detriment
of the people's welfare. When, for example, Rehoboam was
petitioned to lighten the burden placed upon the populace, he
pledged instead, "My father made your yoke heavy, but I will
add to it; my father disciplined you with whips, but I *will discipline you* with scorpions" (2 Chron. 10:14). He hoped thereby
to secure his kingdom; instead the northern tribes were driven
away by his threat.

One can always rationalize oppressive behavior as necessary
to law and order, but not without drawing the prophets' ire.
Jeremiah anticipated a day when all Israel would be as a con-
gregation and the tyrants would be punished for the affliction

they had caused (Jer. 30:20). Whether speaking in international or intranational terms, the prophets sought to prevent the appeal to "national security" from becoming a license for oppression.

We have seen how three antagonists of the prophets (astrology, spiritualism, and misplaced patriotism) have survived and enjoy a contemporary popularity. When fostered by churchmen, this state of affairs only serves to illustrate how far we have strayed from the prophetic emphasis. We may revel in prediction, but we do not take our preparation to meet God as heartily.

A New Tension

I noted that the ancient people were without exception religious and that the prophets called them away from idols to serve the living God. But religion plays a much more subordinate role in most people's lives today, and many have abandoned it altogether. This rise of secularism is without parallel in biblical times.

We seldom appreciate how extensive the change in religious climate has been until we are confronted with a more resistant culture than our own and stop to think how even in this instance the secular spirit has settled in. I read recently that a researcher into extrasensory phenomena commended Chicago as an exceedingly fruitful location for his investigation. The strong ethnic ties of many of the people, he reasoned, made them more open to such possibilities, and therefore occurrences of ESP were more numerous.

This may be so, but Chicago is nevertheless a secular metropolis, and the majority of its inhabitants are a far cry from enjoying the religious sensitivity of ancient people. In Chicago religion appears to be a peripheral concern for many people, or, as some describe it, a leisure activity. I speak here of Chicago only to illustrate what is evident in cities, villages, and rural districts throughout the United States.

We should probably look on secularism as a mixed blessing. On the positive side, it represents something of a deliverance from the ancient idols. However, it can and often does imply new enslavement—out of the frying pan, so to speak, into the fire.

The ancients were forever confusing the gods with nature. A tree might assume a particularly sacred character because it towered over others about it, and sacrifice would be made at its base. The religious groves of asherah were a familiar sight to Israel, and four hundred of their prophets feasted at Jezebel's banquet table (1 Kings 18:20). While Elijah singled out the prophets of Baal for the subsequent contest on Carmel, the prophet took no more kindly to the ministers of Asherah. Elijah clearly meant to desacralize nature as such, to strip it of the idolatry men projected on it. Secularism is, in this sense, a natural result of the prophetic insistence that we rid nature of its gods.

Some of my close friends cringe when I speak in this manner. They feel we should reserve a sense of awe and mystery in regard to nature, and they are likely correct. But the prophets addressed a different subject—the elevation of nature into a pantheon—and this, they warned, is a temptation we must resist.

Ancient rulers also attempted to strengthen their hold on subjects by an appeal to divine right. At one time, the royalty of Egypt insisted that only they were assured of a future life. Even later, one's afterlife was thought to be contingent upon allegiance to those in authority. This trend drew fire from the prophets, likely anticipated by Moses' contest with Pharaoh and certainly refined during the monarchy.

The Hebrew king was never allowed to exempt himself from the stewardship of his office. He ruled, so to speak, by the grace of God. As we noted earlier, Samuel recognized that God had set Saul aside as a result of his abusing the position granted him. No sacred birth or set of circumstances guaranteed his hold on the throne, and so the prophets also desacralized human institutions.

Secularism, inasmuch as it reflects the prophetic protest against natural and civil idolatry, may be thought of as an ally. However, secularism can slam shut our window to heaven, and in that case it would be in league with the opposition to the prophets.

Some years ago I was reading about religion in public education and the positions taken by those debating the issues. It surprised me to find some advocating a rather thorough deletion of religious material while subtly promoting their own secular ideals. They either could not or would not see that for the religious person all life revolves around the Almighty. We can no more turn God off for the duration of the academic day than we can stop breathing. Secularism, for these advocates, had become an alternative to religious belief, guaranteed by the Constitution and safeguarded by judicial precedent. They confused freedom *of* religion with freedom *from* religion.

We cannot produce illustrations from Holy Writ to cover the advent of secularism, but the implication seems clear. The prophet was concerned with revising our thinking in order to give God the place of prominence. Efforts which deny us that possibility collide with the message of the prophets. To the earlier antagonists we add the tendency within secularism to get carried away with its purge of the gods and assault the Almighty as well.

Once a medium attempted to interest me in her predictive ability. "Would you like to know how many children you will have?" she inquired, waiting for a confirmation that never came. No, I preferred to talk about God, his claims, and the obligation they place upon us. She tolerated my preference for a short time, but since she was obviously more interested in probing the future than enjoying the prophetic vision of God, it was perhaps not surprising that our paths never crossed again.

Questions for Study and Discussion

1. How does seeing God as the subject of prophecy influence our understanding? What happens when we fail to keep this focus?

2. Why did the biblical writers cast astrology in such a negative light? How may we account for its persistent popularity and special attraction today?

3. Since spiritualism draws the prophet's rebuke, how do we account for churchmen who pursue it? What counsel would you want them to hear?

4. What distinguishes proper and improper patriotism? Provide examples of each. How would the prophets have spoken to the situations you have selected?

5. In what sense is secularism an ally of the prophets and in what way an enemy? Do you think it is a mixed blessing? Why? Why not?

6. How did the prophets challenge the imposition upon man of nature and human institutions as sacred dictatorships? Were they revolutionaries?

III

Nature of Prophecy [3]

Prophecy never hangs suspended in midair. It reaches out to some audience in a given situation.

> Awake, drunkards, and weep;
> And wail, all you wine drinkers,
> On account of the sweet wine,
> That is cut off from your mouth.

Joel spoke on behalf of God, adding,

> For a nation has invaded my land,
> Mighty and without number;
> Its teeth are the teeth of a lion,
> And it has the fangs of a lioness (Joel 1:5–6).

The prophet acted as a watchman who, having sighted the advancing Babylonian forces, cried out a warning to persons whose callous lives had made them impervious to the danger descending upon them. Sin anesthetizes man to the claims of God, the needs of others, and his own deplorable condition.

Circumstances are not always as obvious as in the case cited, but it is clear that prophecy struggles with man in regard to his obligation. It takes hold and wrestles him into compliance with the will of God.

Prophecy sets before man two options. He can either obey

the commandments of God and be solicitous of the welfare of others, or he can alienate himself from the Almighty by exploiting his fellow man. To be sure, these broad brush strokes are meant not to picture the finer distinctions but simply to outline the basic alternatives. Here the religious theme takes a practical and often painful turn, uncovering our responsibilities and our failure to fulfill them. It indicates man's reluctance to comply with God's design for his life and illustrates the fact that the preferred way does not amble but takes a steady course toward its goal.

Two Ways

"There is a way *which seems* right to man," the sage observed, "but its end is the way of death" (Prov. 14:12). The prophets sensed how easily we blur the difference between God's way and our own. We should be alert to the temptation. When the people in the temple on the Mount of Olives told Jesus, "We are Abraham's offspring, and have never yet been enslaved to anyone," he replied, "Truly, truly, I say to you, every one who commits sin is the slave of sin" (John 8:33–34). A privileged birth, like a good start, will not insure that we run well or finish the race.

An inviting stretch of road provides no better guarantee. Jeremiah contrasted two baskets of figs, the one very good and the other terribly rotten (Jer. 24). Which would represent those left behind after the deportation to Babylon? The good figs, the people thought, but the prophet reported to the contrary. "Thus says the Lord God of Israel, 'Like these good figs, so I will regard as good the captives of Judah, whom I have sent out of this place *into* the land of the Chaldeans'" (Jer. 24:5). God allowed the bad to remain, as though they were not worth the effort to transport. We left them alone with their delusions about righteousness and the favor of God.

We distinguish the two ways by the fruit they bear rather than by some former legacy or present good fortune. Jesus summarized the prophetic opinion: "The tree is known by its fruit" (Matt. 12:33). The psalmist surveyed the two ways: the blessed and the wicked (Ps. 1). The blessed person rejects the company of sinners and scoffers and delights in meditating on the law of God. He or she is like a tree, drawing from a constant supply of water, that brings forth fruit in season. The wicked person differs in every regard; he or she resembles the chaff driven away by the wind. He or she has no place with the righteous in judgment and shall surely perish. These two paths appear before us repeatedly, and we are required to review our choice.

The prophets detailed the behavior we observe as we travel in one direction or the other. Ezekiel commented on personal responsibility:

"What do you mean by using this proverb concerning the land of Israel saying,

> The fathers eat the sour grapes,
> But the children's teeth are set on edge?

'As I live,' declares the Lord God, 'you are surely not going to use this proverb in Israel any more. Behold, all souls are Mine; the soul of the father as well as the soul of the son is Mine. The soul who sins will die' " (Ezek. 18:2–4).

Do not suppose that difficult times befall us simply because the children suffer the iniquity of their fathers, for we must each bear our own guilt. God knows how to take into consideration past influences in dealing with us; we stand or fall as we respond to the options.

Ezekiel looked for road signs: "If a man is righteous, and practices justice and righteousness," if he does not frequent the high places, commit adultery, approach a woman during her menstrual period, oppress anyone, but restores the debtor his pledge, does not commit robbery, gives the hungry bread, the naked clothing, and does not practice usury, but executes true justice, walks in God's statutes and ordinances so as to deal faithfully, then "he is righteous *and* will surely live" (see Ezek. 18:5–9).

We can believe the signs we read along the road, and our behavior should be guided by our own judgment, not by the past actions of our fathers.

The righteous man, Ezekiel continued, "may have a violent son who sheds blood, and who does any of these things to a brother" (those wrongs the prophet has listed). Then "his blood will be on his own head" (see Ezek. 18:10–13).

However, should the wicked man have "a son who has observed all his father's sins which he committed, and observing does not do likewise," the prophet repeated the specifics once more, "when the son has practiced justice and righteousness, and has observed all My statutes and done them, he shall surely live" (see Ezek. 18:14, 19). "The righteousness of the righteous will be upon himself," Ezekiel concluded, "and the wickedness of the wicked will be upon himself" (Ezek. 18:20).

But if the wicked man turns from his sin and observes the statutes and ordinances of God, he will live. The transgressions he has committed will not be remembered because righteousness pushed it aside. "Do I have any pleasure in the death of the wicked," the Almighty wants to know, "rather than that he should turn from his ways and live?" (Ezek. 18:23). God takes no pleasure in the death of anyone.

If, however, the righteous man turns to sin, his righteousness will be forgotten because of the wickedness he commits subsequently. We are left with two ways, and we must decide which road to travel. It is not such a difficult task, as the prophets saw it; one road is marked by thoughtfulness of others and the alternative rides insensitively over their prostrate forms.

The prophets, while first concerned with the religious issue, were also social reformers. They meant to awaken our concern for one another and got pointedly specific in the process. They often identified the offenses people coveted and rationalized. For instance, they uncovered the practice of adultery among those of the dispersion. These people had adhered to the laws when they lived within sight of the temple, when the laws were reinforced by regular instruction, and when they were encouraged to keep the laws by the expectation of others. In the midst of a permissive Babylonian culture, however, they soon forgot these strictures.

The prophets also faulted those who failed to return a pledge of indebtedness (the outer garment meant to protect the man against an evening chill). Business is business, as the saying goes, and one must look out for oneself. Not only for oneself, the prophet would add, but for the welfare of others. We should not crowd out of our minds the thought of that man shivering in the cold, while his wrap serves no purpose but to remind us of a debt.

The offense could also be the result of an omission, as with the failure to provide food for the hungry, either by turning away the request or by simply not being sensitive enough to need. Such sins of omission the prophets blamed on selfish interests which cause an individual to have little or no time for others.

Ezekiel closed his plea, as the prophets were prone to do, with the appeal "therefore, repent and live" (Ezek. 18:32). He bids us to sense the error of our ways and God's will that we mend them; then repent and live.

The Obvious

The prophetic message, again contrary to much popular thought, is a direct, relatively unambiguous declaration of man's responsibilities. It has little patience with subtleties, inferences, connotations, and the like. It tells it like the prophet sees it.

When we find ourselves digging in the prophetic literature for some obscure point, we have almost certainly excavated beyond its intended purpose.

An instance from Elijah's life dramatizes the prophet's candor. When King Ahab saw the prophet, he called out, "Is this you, you troubler of Israel?" (1 Kings 18:17).

"I have not troubled Israel," Elijah flung back at him, "but you and your father's house *have*, because you have forsaken the commandments of the Lord, and you have followed the Baals" (1 Kings 18:18). The prophet provided both case and point: Ahab was the cause of the difficulty, and his recourse to Baal was the means.

Elijah left nothing to conjecture, as was generally characteristic of the prophetic ministry, even when it meant that such a blunt appraisal might jeopardize his life.

Of course, such stalwart behavior could and often did place severe strain on the individual called by God to the prophetic task. Jeremiah protested that he could not manage because of his youthfulness, and the Almighty responded:

> Do not say, "I am a youth,"
> Because everywhere I send you, you shall go,
> And all that I command you, you shall speak.
> Do not be afraid of them,
> For I am with you to deliver you (Jer. 1:7–8).

Do not be intimidated by the task; speak the whole counsel of God; and trust the Almighty to redeem the situation.

The end result of God's preparation of a prophet can be seen in the striking ministry of John the Baptist. Listen as he heralds the Messiah's coming:

> Make ready the way of the Lord,
> Make His paths straight.
> Every ravine shall be filled up,
> And every mountain and hill shall be brought low;

And the crooked shall become straight,
And the rough roads smooth;
And all flesh shall see the salvation of God (Luke 3:4–6; see
    Isa. 40:4–5).

There is no cryptic meaning here, only the bold assertion that they should prepare for the royal visitor's arrival.

But when the multitudes swarmed to hear John, they were met with the jolting inquiry, "You brood of vipers, who warned you to flee from the wrath to come" (Luke 3:7)? This was not the kind of greeting calculated to win friends. "Therefore bring forth fruits in keeping with your repentance," the prophet continued, "and do not begin to say to yourselves, 'We have Abraham for our father,' for I say to you that God is able from these stones to raise up children to Abraham. And also the axe is already laid at the root of the trees; every tree therefore that does not bear good fruit is cut down and thrown into the fire" (Luke 3:8–9). These were certainly plain words, almost belligerent in the way they stripped his listeners of their pertinent qualifications.

The people then began to question John concerning their responsibilities, and they got practical answers. Let those who have two tunics give to someone who has none, so also with your food; let the tax gatherers collect no more than directed; let the soldiers not extort money or bear false witness. Of course, this was not intended to describe all their duties but to pinpoint their nature. The prophets had little love for abstraction, choosing instead to show the more obvious application of their message.

The prophet stopped preaching, as the saying goes, to start meddling. He got into the nitty-gritty where people live and where words have an immediate impact. For instance, the tax collector's profit depended on how much he could gather beyond what must be returned to his superior. If he were to follow John's instruction, his income would be cut back to a modest sum. The soldier also padded his meager wages by bribery and had much to lose by taking the prophet's advice.

It is perhaps not surprising, considering their blunt intrusion into the affairs of others, that the prophets' trail should be marked with violence. "O Jerusalem, Jerusalem, who kills the prophets and stones those who are sent to her," Jesus lamented over the city, "how often I wanted to gather your children together, the way a hen gathers her chicks under her wings, and you were unwilling" (Matt. 23:37). Instead Jerusalem preferred to continue its blood bath.

The Not So Obvious

We may, however, be misled by the prophet's seeming preference for speaking in specific terms. His solutions were seldom cut and dried; they left considerable latitude for God to work. He wanted to creatively open up new possibilities.

We are often given the impression that sin is new. On the contrary, sin follows predictable patterns, well worn by former clients. Sin seems to take to the ruts where little personal initiative or restraint is called for.

"Awake, drunkards, and weep," Joel admonished his hearers, "and wail, all you wine drinkers" (Joel 1:5). He painted the portrait of someone in a drunken stupor brought on by the practice of sin. The drunkard thought of himself as alert, but he was really dull and unresponsive, not the life of the party but a thorough bore.

Shake off the effects of drink, Joel encouraged the drunkard, clear your mind and get in on the exciting things God means to bring about. Be awake to the opportunities.

Hosea described Israel's unrepentant ways in monotonous, repetitive language. He reported that

> The more they [the prophets] called them,
> The more they went from them;

> They kept sacrificing to the Baals
> And burning incense to idols (Hos. 11:2)

even though, as Hosea added, God taught them to walk in the first place. Hosea suggested that the people had turned that fresh experience with God into a humdrum life of sin.

Who can say what marvelous things await those who turn to the Almighty? God promises to love them freely (Hos. 14:4), and love takes any number of creative avenues. Love is the most unpredictable of virtues because it sets the welfare of its object above its own reputation. It volunteers what duty could never imagine to require.

I recall an elderly couple whose life together had matured into one of those exceptionally rich relationships. I could not speak their language, nor they mine; so I was free to observe more carefully than would otherwise have been the case, and I was thoroughly impressed with their loving concern for each other. So it is for those who experience God's love; we never know what creative course it will take next.

God's way resembles the dawn of a new day. Yesterday grew weary and tired, and we put it to rest in order to greet the first streak of light as it touched the sky. We get a new lease on life, an alternative laden with possibilities. "This is the day which the Lord has made," assured the psalmist, "let us rejoice and be glad in it" (Ps. 118:24). The prospect appears as encouraging as God's imaginative compassion.

But the prophet had to contend with circumstances which seemed to curtail God's working. Often Israel had been subjected to foreign powers or suffered from the affliction of her own rulers. The rich conspired against the poor. Religion was slow to plead the cause of those refused justice. One did not have to search far for a reason to despair.

These circumstances were driven home for Jeremiah when he visited the potter's house (Jer. 18:1–12). The vessel the potter turned upon his wheel was marred, and he began to fashion another one to take its place. "Can I not, O house of Israel, deal with you as this potter *does*?" declared the Almighty. "Behold, like the clay in the potter's hand, so are you in My hand, O house of Israel" (Jer. 18:6). For all of that, Jeremiah was warned that people would think the matter hopeless and opt to stay with the spoiled situation.

An imperfect vessel seems better than none at all if we assume we can get nothing better to replace it. Thus the thinking went, and with such the prophets struggled. Cannot God deal with us as the potter does with his clay? Imagine those artistic hands deftly moving about the spinning lump of clay until it rises a vessel anyone would rejoice to have grace his home.

On a number of occasions I have watched the potter at work. His clay reveals nothing of what lies within his creative imagination, what he intends to make or how he proposes to bring it to pass. But soon he has the vessel completed and set aside to bake in his oven. Can God do less?

I have also watched the artless efforts of those inexperienced in the potter's trade. They usually fail to implement their idea. Should we suppose God so devoid of talent when it comes to working with us?

The prophet was committed to making God known, not as some blundering buffoon but as a thoroughly skilled artisan—so skilled, in fact, that the talented potter's efforts would seem as inept as the novice's in comparison.

The prophet's audience was encouraged to assume the qualities of clay: to be pliable, flexible, usable. Clay does not resist the potter's efforts the way that Israel was prone to defy the Almighty.

I have a small clay pitcher, reported to be from the time of King David. The potter was not especially gifted if we can assume this to be representative of his work. His lack of expertise notwithstanding, it seems remarkable that we should have this continuing memorial to his craft, made possible as the clay yielded to his entreaty.

What precisely might God do with people so accommodated to his will? The prophet's answer became more vague at this point than when he described the two ways we may travel. He intimated one thing, offered us a glimpse of something else, but never got around to spelling out just how the potter will choose to mold those individuals pliable to his touch. Time will tell, but for now the important thing is to get on the right track.

While prophecy is primarily a religious activity, it has profound social implications. It demands that we get right with God, but it also urges us to become reconciled with one another. In the latter connection, prophecy is painfully obvious in its references to what we should or should not be doing, but when it comes to unfolding the limitless possibilities for a life yielded to God, it avoids getting down to specifics. We can never presume to know what marvelous form the Almighty's love may take.

Prophecy establishes a tension between the will of God and the ways of man. While the former may at times seem an imposition or an inconvenience, it is to man's advantage to abide by it. While the latter may appear at first inviting, it proves to be a difficult alternative, filled with obstacles and ending in utter loss. Prophecy prescribes a binary choice, not between God and man, but between God/man and sin (which prohibits us from striding together through time and eternity). "Do two men walk together unless they have made an appointment?" (Amos 3:3). No? Then, the prophets urged, be reconciled to God.

Questions for Study and Discussion

1. Define *prophecy*. Do you feel your definition is biblical? What alternative definitions of prophecy do you know of?

2. Might the prophets be thought of as watchmen whose warnings pierce the night? Can you think of other descriptive analogies that would define their role?

3. What justification is there for the idea that the prophets invited men to love God and their neighbor? Is there any other basic theme to their proclamations?

4. What may mislead us into thinking that God is pleased with our disregard of his will? How did the prophets attempt to alert their audience to this miscalculation?

5. Were the prophets social reformers? Were they only social reformers?

6. Would you agree that the prophets meant to clarify for, instead of confound, their listeners? Can you suggest illustrations in addition to those mentioned in this chapter?

7. What accounts for the more ambiguous utterances of the prophets? Would you challenge those reasons submitted in this discussion or include some which were not?

8. Prophecy requires a binary (one out of two) choice, "not between God and man, but between God/man and sin." How do you react to this statement? Against what misconception does it mean to warn us?

IV

Context of Prophecy

God is the subject of prophecy, man is its target, and the message is an invitation to a creative relationship between the two. Prophecy primarily occurs in connection with the instruction of a select people, as preparation for the coming of Messiah.

It is customary to list the prophets from Moses to John the Baptist (Luke 7:28), but Abraham was also called a prophet (Gen. 20:7). Enoch too was said to have prophesied (Jude 14). That Abraham, the father of the prophets, should have anticipated them seems sensible enough, but the case of Enoch is so obscure that one hesitates to speculate on it. The reference may be to a source bearing his name rather than to the ancient figure we associate with the name.

Nor can we strictly say that prophecy concluded with John the Baptist. Jesus was identified as *That* prophet (John 1:21, 6:14; Acts 3:23), a messianic term which suggests that he embodied the prophetic ministry as he did the priestly function (Heb. 2:17) and the role of a sage (1 Cor. 1:24). But Jesus should be thought of as one *with* the prophets rather than one *of* the prophets, as when Paul referred to the death of Jesus *and* the prophets (1 Thess. 2:14).

More to the point, prophecy persisted in the early church

(probably not with critical importance and likely with diminishing frequency). Paul even encouraged the Corinthians in regard to prophecy, although in reference to their excitement over speaking in tongues (1 Cor. 14:1–3, 39).

Scripture implies that there was a time before God spoke through the prophets as well as a later period when he superseded them with his Son: "God, after He spoke long ago to the fathers in the prophets in many portions and in many ways, in these last days has spoken to us in *His* Son" (Heb. 1:1–2). There are thus three eras—preprophetic, prophetic, and postprophetic.

Preprophetic

Some knowledge of God preceded the prophets. Paul asserted: "For since the creation of the world His invisible attributes, His eternal power and divine nature, have been clearly seen, being understood through what has been made, so that they are without excuse" (Rom. 1:20). Paul commented to the Lystran Gentiles that God had not left himself "without witness, in that He did good and gave you rains from heaven and fruitful seasons, satisfying your hearts with food and gladness" (Acts 14:17). Upon observing an Athenian altar inscribed to an unknown god, he announced, "What therefore you worship in ignorance, this I proclaim to you" (Acts 17:23). God's signature was written broadly across the heavens long before the prophets made their entrance.

The apostle sensed power but not as a property of nature, a blind force, an evolutionary urge. It resulted from God's determination to press his purposes, as Habakkuk wrote:

> He stood and surveyed the earth;
> He looked and startled the nations.
> Yes, the perpetual mountains were shattered,

The ancient hills collapsed.
His ways are everlasting (Hab. 3:6).

The nations were alarmed at his approach; their defenses no longer seemed secure. Under the tread of God's feet, the earth also trembled until those proud hills, which had stood the ravages of time, shook themselves apart and bowed before their Creator. Thus the prophet picked up the threads others had prepared for him to weave into a more intricate design.

I have found it helpful to think of this preprophetic revelation of God in terms of his hounding and haunting man.

Where can I go from Thy Spirit?
Or where can I flee from Thy presence?
If I ascend to heaven, Thou art there;
If I make my bed in Sheol, behold, Thou art there.
If I take the wings of the dawn,
If I dwell in the remotest part of the sea,
Even there Thy hand will lead me,
And Thy right hand will lay hold of me (Ps. 139:7–10).

The hunt is on, man the fox and God the hound. It is a hopeless contest, the psalmist concluded, God getting the better of us.

Habukkuk spoke of the nations as being startled, spooked by God's approach. Meaning no irreverence, the Holy Ghost might be described as the Holy Spook. He sends those eerie quivers up and down our spines and makes our hair stand on end.

Let us return to Paul's Lystran experience as a case in point. The uproar began at the healing of a cripple. "The gods have become like men and have come down to us," the shocked observers cried out, supposing Barnabas to be Zeus and Paul, his spokesman Hermes. The apostles could hardly restrain the excited citizens from offering sacrifices to them on the spot. Their emotions were as faultless as their understanding was faulty; indeed, God haunted them!

Merge the metaphors of hound and haunt, and we see that Paul was accurate in stating that God "is not far from each one of us; for in Him we live and move and exist" (Acts 17:27–28). The Almighty is here, so much so that we keep bumping into him; this was true even in the times before the prophets.

What tends to happen in such an instance can be seen in the so-called primitive religions; God retreats in favor of our working with his subordinates. He becomes the high God, relatively removed, deferred to in exceptional cases, but seldom with the assurance that he will intervene. He is appealed to as a last, desperate resort when all else has failed, and sometimes in resignation to the inscrutable ways he works. The pantheon moves in to negotiate with us in the areas vacated by the high God; these gods receive the primitive's attentions, his sacrifices, rituals, and customs.

Eugene Nida has documented the fact that more sophisticated societies operate in much the same way, lacking some corrective. They turn to astrology and spiritualism when great creedal truths lose significance. The pantheon, in one form or another, comes rushing in to fill the vacuum created by the collapse of vital life-signs.

This suggests that for all practical purposes many still live in the preprophetic era. They have turned the pages back to earlier chapters of man's existence. Far from giving a hearing to the Son, they have also hushed the prophets. As a Theosophist boasted to me: "Yes, we prefer antiquity and life rooted in previous times." She was happy over the prospect, but she would not have found Paul a genial companion. We "preach the gospel to you in order that you should turn from these vain things to a living God" (Acts 14:15), he explained to the Lystrans. In his correspondence to Rome, the apostle spoke of the emptiness, the fruitlessness, and the willfulness of a belief that "exchanged the glory of the incorruptible God for an image in the form of corruptible man and of birds and four-footed animals and crawling creatures" (Rom. 1:23). It is a preference which persists into our times and is not without consequences for our behavior. "For this reason God gave them over to degrading passions" (Rom. 1:26), Paul added, along with some details of what he had in mind. The Almighty tolerated this situation in "the times of ignorance" but now declares "to men that all everywhere should repent" (Acts 17:30). The postprophetic is thus defined as an era when men sense God's presence but are inclined to turn it to idolatry and an occasion for wickedness.

Prophetic

God introduced the prophets to a chosen people over an extended period of time as a corrective of past abuses and to unfold his truths more exactly. We must accustom ourselves to think in terms of a select people who became the means of God's blessing all mankind.

Israel was encouraged from the outset to discriminate among those who professed to be prophets. Seers were to speak only what God commanded them and what would therefore come to pass (Deut. 18:19–22), that is, subsequent prophetic messages should be consistent with the Law, as given by the prophet Moses, and should correctly identify God's continued working. The Law was the treaty, or covenant, assumed by any faithful prophet and was binding whatever the future circumstances. This helps explain the vigorous debate between Jesus and his opposition in reference to the Law.

God does not say one thing today and the reverse tomorrow. His words continue to echo down through the corridors of time, each addition blending into the remainder.

I once climbed to the site where Moses is said to have received the Law. Looking down on the surrounding peaks, I mused that no prophet, figuratively speaking, climbed higher than Moses. Each had to settle for a lower summit; each had to be content with being part of the range dominated by the peak upon which the Law was given.

A faithful prophet also had to speak the truth about the existing situation or the one that was about to develop, but this should not lead us to believe that prediction was all-important for the prophets. When we say the prophet must be truthful, we mean he must faithfully represent God at work and Man's responsibility in that connection. The prophet might refer to some future event, but his words must truly espress God's continuing activity.

Take Jesus' condemnation of certain "scribes and Pharisees, hypocrites" (Matt. 23:13–15, 23, 25, 27, 29) as an example. They intended to represent Moses, but they so misread the situation as to distort the Law and make a mockery of prophecy. As long as they continued to rob others and indulge themselves, they would never be companions to the prophets.

Jesus characterized the "weightier provisions of the law" as "justice and mercy and faithfulness" (Matt. 13:23)—justice and mercy toward our fellow men, faithfulness in regard to the Almighty. What is not cut from that design has no business being patched into the prophet's robe.

But, turning first to Micah, let the prophets speak for themselves on the matter:

> He has told you, O man, what is good;
> And what does the Lord require of you
> But to do justice, to love kindness,
> And to walk humbly with your God (Mic. 6:8)?

The prophets dwelt on the subject of justice to such a degree that we can read their words in that light. They spoke of the need for justice, its lack, God's concern, impending judgment—one could almost "predict" the direction their comments would take.

Daniel, drawn to a related concern, warned Nebuchadnezzar to "break away now from your sins by *doing* righteousness, and from your iniquities by showing mercy to *the* poor" (Dan. 4:27). Justice, the prophet appears to suggest, needs a helping hand from compassion. Equity falls short when people cannot reach out to accept it. In such a situation it suffers like the retarded child who cannot keep pace in a class of normal children and develops severe emotional problems in the process. A more compassionate solution is called for.

Justice and mercy walk hand in hand through the prophet's message. They stand in opposition to what had often been the practice and continued to be among the nations about them. The prophets called for Israel, the people of God and the servant of God to others, to embrace justice and mercy as national goals.

The emphasis also looked forward to the coming of *that* prophet who would embody the ideals the prophets now struggled to realize. Moses promised: "The Lord your God will raise up for you a prophet like me from among you, from your countrymen, you shall listen to him" (Deut. 18:15; see Acts 3:22–23). The prophets sensed that they were a preparation for one yet to come. Their message would be accented at a future time, their periods turned into exclamation points.

However, justice and mercy are cast in a religious context. They prove elusive ideals when stalked for their own sake; as we walk humbly with the Almighty, justice and mercy are cultivated in the fertile soil of our love for him.

The prophets' task was to turn men from idols to serve the living God, to observe justice and mercy as a matter of devotion to him, and to anticipate the arrival of *that* prophet. From Moses to John the Baptist, the prophets linked the wayward people and the faithful prophet to come. Their frustrating effort was made easier by realizing that what they sowed, another would reap to the everlasting glory of God and the blessing of all those who diligently seek him.

Postprophetic

While some persist in living in preprophetic days, others prefer prophetic to postprophetic times. They resist the transition from the prophets to the Son.

John the Baptist viewed matters differently when he concluded, "He [Jesus] must increase, but I must decrease" (John 3:30). That decision was not only appropriate for him but for all prophets. "I am not the Christ," John had admitted, "but, I have been sent before Him. He who has the bride is the bridegroom; but the friend of the bridegroom, who stands and hears him, rejoices greatly because of the bridegroom's voice. And so this joy of mine has been made full" (John 3:28–29).

Jesus, for his part, observed that "the Law and the Prophets *were* proclaimed until John; since then the gospel of the kingdom of God is preached and every one is forcing his way into it" (Luke 16:16). And again the Master commented, "I say to you, among those born of women, there is no one greater than John; yet he who is least in the kingdom of God is greater than he" (Luke 7:28). A critical point has been reached in God's strategy. We have left the "long ago" and entered the "last days," as the Book of Hebrews contrasts the two, leaving the era of the prophets for that of the Son.

Prophets continued to minister within the early church. A variety of explanations have been given to account for that situation. Some interpreters prefer to phase out the prophets, preferably sooner than later, and have them eliminated by the time the first generation of Christians passes from the scene. Others consider the prophets a mark of the last days, highlighting the prophecy of Joel (Joel 2:28–32; see Acts 2:17–21). I suspect both overstate the case.

Although the available evidence is less than conclusive, it has been established that Jesus superceded the prophets in relationship to the last days, Jesus' ministry in the last days was to some degree extended through a select apostolic group. Thus we understand the unique role these men enjoyed in the church. "I have many more things to say to you, but you cannot bear *them* now," Jesus told them. "But when He, the Spirit of truth, comes, He will guide you into all the truth" (John 16:12–13). Such guidance was to be provided, not only for their benefit, but for ours. The early church sensed this peculiar relationship through the apostles in a way that subsequent generations have found difficult. For instance, the inclusion of material as Scripture hinged in part on whether it enjoyed apostolic sponsorship.

But when we follow the account of the first Christians, we see that the role of the apostle soon weakened in favor of leaders who bore no such special relationship to Jesus. The apostles seemed to have acted like a midwife to assure the birth of the infant church.

The prophets were more incidental to the early church than the apostles. There are references to a company of prophets from Jerusalem (Acts 11:28), one of their number (Agabus) making a second appearance (Acts 21:10), and Paul's instruction concerning prophecy at Corinth. The biblical record also contains a few passing allusions, but even taken together, these passages do not provide a very impressive array. Only when we try to make the Corinthian instance normative, a questionable undertaking in light of the abuses Paul was addressing, does prophecy seem to play a critical role. Otherwise, it slips quietly into the background.

I doubt, however, that we can rule out the possibility of prophecy as some have chosen to do. Paul's comment that love will persist after prophecy, tongues, and knowledge pass away (1 Cor. 13:8) seems less than conclusive support. And prophecy's continuance, however marginal, along with the apostle's commendation, even though he contrasts it with the lesser importance of tongues, warns us not to jump to a hasty conclusion.

But neither should prophecy gain the kind of prominence it rightfully enjoyed before being *digested* by *that* Prophet. Jesus speaks to us today, and the prophets have precious little to say to us that Jesus did not discuss in his ministry. They should volunteer to retire, to decrease in importance, as did John the Baptist, that Christ might be preeminent. They should take to heart the instruction given those who saw Jesus transfigured and after Peter offered to build booths for Jesus, Moses, and Elijah. A voice spoke out of the cloud, saying, "This is My beloved Son, with whom I am well-pleased; hear Him" (Matt. 17:5). It is not Moses, the representative of the Law, we are instructed to hear, nor is it Elijah, the representative of the prophets, but Jesus, the spokesman for these latter days.

This is not to say that prophecy is less significant now when rightly understood. The prophetic themes climb the Mount of Transfiguration with Jesus to gain a new dimension and importance for our day. What remains in doubt is the place of prophec*ies* today. The following story illustrates the point. I gathered along with some two hundred people one spring morning under the arching branches of a massive tree. An opportunity was given us to share what might be of encouragement to others, and one girl announced that she, a prophetess, had a message from God for those assembled. She spoke, paraphrasing Scripture and applying it as a gentle reprimand and qualified commendation. Nothing she said, as nearly as I could determine, was enhanced by declaring her words as a prophecy, except that she spoke in the first person (for God) rather than third person (for herself).

Had she understood the place of prophecy or her role in relation to it? I have no way of being certain, but I suspect that she was ill-advised. I would be more inclined to expect such a gift to be exercised, if at all, in a situation where the truths of Scripture were little known or possibly badly distorted. Neither of these conditions existed, according to the girl's own estimation of the situation.

What then is the place of prophecy? It lays the preparation for that final word spoken by Jesus Christ, and it lives on, not in competition with Jesus, but primarily as its great truths become part of our thoughts, motivations, and actions. It schools us in Christ.

Questions for Study and Discussion

1. What is the role of prophecy in the progressive revelation of God? How would our understanding suffer without it?

2. How does the preprophetic attitude evidence itself today? Discuss specific examples.

3. Read Deuteronomy 18:19–22. First discuss the meaning of this passage if prophecy is defined as foretelling. Now consider the passage with prophecy defined as forthtelling.

4. What are the "weightier provisions of the law" as outlined by Jesus?

5. I take a position which allows the possibility of prophecy today although I believe its uses are limited. Do you agree or disagree? On what basis?

6. Reflect on the idea that "the prophetic themes climb the Mount of Transfiguration with Jesus to gain a new dimension and importance for our day." What is this significance of subordinating prophecy to Christ?

7. Have you encountered self-proclaimed prophets? How did you deal with their claims?

V

Leverage of Prophecy

The prophets moved earth by way of heaven. Isaiah had a vision the year King Uzziah died of "the Lord sitting on a throne, lofty and exalted, with the train of His robe filling the temple" (Isa. 6:1). This portrait of an oriental monarch is in keeping with the imagery the prophets associated with the kingdom of God.

The events of Uzziah's reign strengthened the impact of Isaiah's vision. The king had begun to rule at the age of sixteen and continued for fifty-two years, during which time he organized and equipped a strong military force, fortified the country, and extended its boundaries. Then, driven by pride, he usurped the priest's prerogatives to offer incense at the temple and was struck down with leprosy. Uzziah, after years of faithful service, violated his vassal relationship to the great King.

The words of William Doane, nineteenth-century poet, come to mind here:

> Ancient of Days, who sittest throned in glory,
> To Thee all knees are bent, all voices pray;
> Thy love has blessed the wide world's wondrous story
> With light and life since Eden's dawning day.

God reigns, rewards our faithfulness, and judges our offenses.

Isaiah, in contrast to Uzziah, was overcome with a sense of unworthiness and lamented:

> . . . I am a man of unclean lips,
> And I live among a people of unclean lips;
> For my eyes have seen the King, the Lord of hosts (Isa. 6:5).

Then one of the seraphim, who ministered to the great King, flew to Isaiah with a burning coal taken from the altar, touched Isaiah's mouth, and said, "Behold, this has touched your lips; and your iniquity is taken away, and your sin is forgiven" (Isa. 6:7).

Isaiah next overheard the Almighty pondering who he might send to bear his message, and he offered, "Here am I. Send me!" (Isa. 6:8). So the great King dispatched Isaiah to bring a word which would harden those who heard it, and, as the chronicler succinctly put it, "the people continued acting corruptly" (2 Chron. 27:2). "Lord, how long?" the prophet asked, wishing to know how long this condition would continue. Until they shall be dispersed, the great King replied, leaving but a faithful remnant.

We have listened in on the call of a prophet and sensed that it related to the sovereign rule of God. It is a magnificent perspective that makes much contemporary discussion of prophecy seem like child's play. We behold a breathtaking vista of the Kingdom of God.

Kingdom in Fact

Isaiah saw the Almighty ruling in spite of Uzziah's presumptive act, the close of an otherwise positive reign, and the warning against increased callousness. Home base, in a manner of speaking, remained strong even when the vassal relationship weakened appreciably.

The psalmist provided a classic expression of this theme (Ps. 2). The nations arouse themselves to join forces against the great King. They encourage one another to tear off the fetters and cast them aside, their shouts building into an unholy uproar. At which

> He who sits in the heavens laughs,
> The Lord scoffs at them.
> Then He will speak to them in His anger
> And terrify them in His fury (Ps. 2:4–5).

How ridiculous that such puny creatures would imagine they could challenge the Almighty! Their chariots would fold from his breath, the legions melt from his gaze, their words drop short of their target like so many spent arrows. Come along and see if you can do better; bellow louder, beat your shields, breach heaven's ramparts with your siege equipment. Then, a pause, as if to wait for some new effort, and an admonition:

> Now therefore, O kings, show discernment;
> Take warning, O judges of the earth.
> Worship the Lord with reverence,
> And rejoice with trembling (Ps. 2:10–11).

Recall your treaty obligations before it is too late and you perish before the anger of the great King.

This point of view helps us understand the courage expressed by the apostles when hauled before the Sanhedrin and given strict orders not to teach in the name of Jesus. "We must obey God," they replied, "rather than men" (Acts 5:29). It was better to risk their safety with the tribunal than to break faith with the Almighty. Jesus drew upon the same imagery: "Do not fear those who kill the body, but are unable to kill the soul; but rather fear Him who is able to destroy both soul and body in hell" (Matt. 10:28).

Given God's sovereignty, he sometimes seemed to keep a

loose rein on the wicked and to be in no hurry to deliver the righteous. The psalmist's reaction reveals a similar view:

> My God, my God, why hast Thou forsaken me?
> Far from my deliverance are the words of my groaning.
> O my God, I cry by day, but Thou dost not answer;
> And by night, but I have no rest (Ps. 22:1–2).

Then his thoughts turn backward to the legacy of his people, how God rescued them time and again from their enemies.

> In Thee our fathers trusted;
> They trusted, and Thou didst deliver them.
> To Thee they cried out, and were delivered;
> In Thee they trusted, and were not disappointed (Ps. 22:4–5).

But what of him? He seems more a worm than a man, reproached, despised, mocked, taunted.

> Yet Thou art He who didst bring me forth from the womb;
> Thou didst make me trust *when* upon my mother's breasts
> (Ps. 22:9).

The recollection is short lived, for trouble comes upon him like strong bulls on every side and as a ravenous and roaring lion. His inner resolve weakens like wax melting before a flame.

So the psalmist cried out for deliverance and lived to recite God's faithfulness in the sanctuary, and the prophets developed what some have thought to be a solitary spirit, a resolve which seemed at times to invite the rage of others or earn their grudging respect.

Jeremiah helps us sum up:

> But the Lord is the true God;
> He is the living God and the everlasting King.
> At His wrath the earth quakes,
> And the nations cannot endure His indignation (Jer. 10:10).

The kingdom of God, alluded to here, knows neither beginning nor end. We challenge it at our risk. While rebels may seem to get the better of things at the moment, God knows how to grind out judgment and deliver those who trust in him. The prophet exemplifies a stalwart determination which prefers the martyr's lot to the lavish courts of the wicked.

This determination provides life with a leverage, a purchase outside itself that cannot be altered by the prosperity, defection, or demise of Uzziah. It is with this resolve that the prophetic ministry originates, that it finds its strength and its dynamic. "I saw the Lord sitting on a throne, lofty and exalted"; these are the words that set biblical prophecy on its demanding course.

Kingdom at Hand

A certain New Testament teacher likes to begin his first class session with a question concerning the subject of Jesus' teaching. He seldom gets the answer he wants immediately and is sometimes forced to lead into it with a generous hint. Scripture, however, is quite clear on the matter. Like John the Baptist before him, Jesus took up the refrain "Repent, for the kingdom of heaven is at hand" (Matt. 4:17).

Handed a scroll of Isaiah as he entered the synagogue at Nazareth, Jesus located the passage which reads:

> The Spirit of the Lord God is upon me,
> Because the Lord has anointed me—
> To bring good news to the afflicted;
> He has sent me to bind up the brokenhearted,
> To proclaim liberty to captives,
> And freedom to prisoners;
> To proclaim the favorable year of the Lord (Isa. 61:1–2).

Here the Master set aside the text to announce the fulfillment of the prophecy. The kingdom was at hand.

Soon Jesus was gathering disciples, and he set out to instruct them (Matt. 5–7). "Blessed are the poor in spirit," he confided, "for theirs is the kingdom of heaven" (Matt. 5:3). Blessed also are those who mourn, the gentle, those who hunger and thirst for righteousness, the merciful, the pure in heart, the peacemakers, and those persecuted for the sake of righteousness. "Rejoice, and be glad, for your reward in heaven is great," the Lord concluded, "for so they persecuted the prophets who were before you" (Matt. 5:12).

Jesus often chose to teach in parables, and so one day he described the sowing of a field and how some seeds fell beside the road and birds came and devoured them. Some fell on rocky places where there was little soil, and lacking root they withered under the scorching sun. Others settled among thorns and were choked out; still others landed on good ground and enjoyed a varied yield (Matt. 13:3–8). The disciples asked Jesus to explain his preference for parables. "To you it has been granted to know the mysteries of the kingdom of heaven," he replied, "but to them it has not been granted" (Matt. 13:11). Here Jesus quotes from God's commissioning of Isaiah, as justification for confirming the people in their callousness. The meaning of the kingdom and the message of prophecy are consistent, from Isaiah through the ministry of Jesus.

On occasion the Master called attention to the meager beginnings of the kingdom and its glorious end. It resembles a mustard seed, he observed, which grows so as to support the birds in its branches (Matt. 13:31–32). The seed also acts like leaven causing bread to raise (Matt. 13:33). Its unpretentious start belies the final impressive result.

"Now having been questioned by the Pharisees as to when the kingdom of God was coming, He answered them and said, 'The kingdom of God is not coming with signs to be observed; nor will they say, "Look, here it is!" or, "There it is!" For behold, the kingdom of God is in your midst'" (Luke 17:20–21). They hoped to procrastinate a bit longer while Jesus cautioned them that time had run out.

"How hard it is for those who are wealthy to enter the kingdom of God!" Jesus mused so that all might hear. "For it is easier for a camel to go through the eye of a needle, than for a rich man to enter the kingdom of God" (Luke 18:24–25). "For where your treasure is," the Master had observed earlier, "there will your heart be also" (Luke 12:34).

"The kingdom of heaven is like a merchant seeking fine pearls," Jesus noticed, "and upon finding one pearl of great value, he went and sold all that he had, and bought it" (Matt. 13:45–46). Jesus counsels us not to hesitate to pay the cost, seeing how valuable the purchase is.

With many other exhortations Jesus urged his listeners to embrace the kingdom. The kingdom of God was at hand, somehow much nearer than previously, within reach, only a child's response away. But it still might be that we would readily reject it as did those in Isaiah's day, either deliberately, by postponing the decision to a more opportune time, or because we are obsessed with the affairs of this world.

We are left to determine how Jesus' announcement that the kingdom is at hand and in our midst has changed things since the time of Isaiah. The most obvious difference relates to the Lord himself; the Messiah has come!

We need only return to the imagery of John the Baptist to highlight the nature of Jesus' arrival. John had enjoined the multitude, streaming out into the wilderness to hear his words, to prepare the way for a royal visitor: Make the way level, set everything in order, the Messiah comes! Now the herald's promise had come to pass. The Christ and in that respect the kingdom had arrived.

We may also look at the matter from the opposite direction. Jesus said, "I always do the things that are pleasing to Him" (John 8:29). The will of God was perfectly realized in Jesus, and one cannot ask for a better demonstration of the kingdom than that.

The kingdom of God, in a manner of speaking, was fleshed out in Jesus. This was true as regards who he was, the obedience he practiced, and his ministry. "What kind of a man is this," they marveled, "that even the winds and the sea obey Him?" (Matt. 8:27). Jesus' healing of the infirm produced similar astonishment, and when John's disciples asked to be assured that Jesus was the Messiah, he let the works speak for themselves. He bore the good news to the afflicted, bound up the brokenhearted, proclaimed liberty to the captives, freed those imprisoned, and declared the favorable year of the Lord.

As a result, the world has never recovered its former composure. Jesus left a company of followers who have adopted many of his characteristics. For instance, they choose to suffer rather than deny the great King, and they try to serve others as Jesus did.

Paul identified this group as Christ's body (Eph. 4:12). They are, to carry out the implications of the metaphor, his feet and hands. They represent to the world, although imperfectly, the kingdom in capsule form.

Some virtually equate the church with the kingdom, at least for the present, but that does not follow. Christ's coming set in motion something greater than the church itself, a "favorable year" and a hardening of resistance as well.

The positive response to Christ can be seen in at least two connections (in addition to the Christian fellowship) as his teaching molds the perspective of men and governs their behavior. One can cultivate a Christian way of thinking about life, short of conversion. You would never know that such a person lacks a personal commitment, except for his or her own comment or that of another. He or she better exemplifies those traits associated with Jesus than do most church people in the community. While such cases may be relatively rare, the Christian perspective has invaded our thinking more extensively than most realize.

Jesus' influence also extends into areas of personal and corporate behavior. I cringe when I hear someone refer to the United States as a Christian nation, but the concept bears an element of truth. Our laws, ordinances, and expectations reflect a Christian orientation. For instance, we disallow polygamy by law, restrict Sunday activity by ordinance, and encourage heterosexuality by general consensus.

This impact on thought and action provides a more favorable climate for us to live in and is more conducive to gaining a favorable response to Christ from individuals. However, Jesus indicated that his ministry would cause persons to harden their resistance and increase their waywardness. This might be illustrated by such extreme cases as someone's writing a book on why I am not a Christian or going to the trouble to prepare a ritual by reversing the words of the Lord's Prayer. Much overreaction to Christian inconsistencies may fall into the same pattern.

What we have said up to this point resembles more the symptoms of the kingdom of God as viewed in light of Christ's advent rather than the case itself. The fact is God exercises his sovereign rule in light of the coming of Christ; it is both the favorable year and the formidable threat associated with the latter days. Isaiah sensed the flow of the current, but the kingdom burst into rapids with Christ's advent. It will carry along those who commit their ways to the surging waters or capsize those struggling against them.

Kingdom in Prospect

Jesus reserved some aspects of the kingdom for the future. "There will be weeping and gnashing of teeth there when you see Abraham and Isaac and Jacob and all the prophets in the kingdom of God, and yourselves being cast out," the Master warned, adding that some "will come from east and west, and from north and south, and will recline *at table* in the kingdom of God" (Luke 13:28–29). The day of judgment and reclamation remains in the future.

Now evil thrashes about as if it had been struck a mortal blow and is bent on as much havoc as possible in the time remaining. It strikes out first in one direction and then another, driven by desperation, heedless of its victims' cries.

Jesus stopped pointedly short in reading the Isaiah scroll with reference to "the day of vengeance of our God" (Isa. 61:2). That day of reckoning must wait a while longer, not as an indefinite postponement but as an additional act of clemency. Peter meant to put the matter in proper perspective: "The Lord is not slow about His promise, as some count slowness, but is patient toward you, not wishing for any to perish but for all to come to repentance" (2 Pet. 3:9).

The peace of God also lingers. That marvelous word *shalom* signifies well-being, health, vigor, blessing—all the benefits of the kingdom rolled into one, as conveyed by persons drawn from all corners of the world to enjoy the banquet table of the great King.

The imagery predates newspapers and television and recalls a time when news was communicated by the traveler in the course of his wanderings. It lodged with him by night and was carried to a distant village before it was repeated to a new group of eager listeners. While God has been working in the lives of persons separated by distance and time, the table allows them to share their reports with one another. Imagine the excitement provided by such an interchange!

We may also dwell on the table creaking under the strain of tempting portions. You may receive many invitations during your lifetime, some to a scanty fare and others more satisfying. None could begin to compare with the table set by the great King.

The Host, more than anyone or anything else, makes the

invitation fascinating. To be asked to sit at table with the Almighty seems to captivate the imagination to the point where one wonders how there could be time for or interest in anything else. Where do we place the emphasis in that verse, on those coming from contrasting directions, on the table, or on the gracious Benefactor? I suppose on the last.

To sum up, the kingdom of God figured largely in the prophetic ministry. It was the underlying conviction which gave rise to prophecy in the first place, sustained it under often difficult circumstances, became the burden of Jesus' calling, and framed the anticipation for the future. When Daniel had made an end of surveying the kingdoms yet to come, he announced that "in the days of those kings the God of heaven will set up a kingdom which will never be destroyed, and *that* kingdom will not be left for another people; it will crush and put an end to all these kingdoms, but it will itself endure forever" (Dan. 2:44). Obadiah likewise affirmed that

> The deliverers will ascend Mount Zion
> To judge the mountain of Esau,
> And the kingdom will be the Lord's (Obad. 21).

The prophets never believed that breaking the treaty with the great King subverted his sovereign rule. In due time the land would be reclaimed and bring in the enduring peace of God.

Their anticipation took the form of enthusiastic flights of oratory, as with Isaiah:

> And He will judge between the nations,
> And will render decisions for many peoples;
> And they will hammer their swords into plowshares, and their
>   spears into pruning hooks.
> Nation will not lift up sword against nation,
> And never again will they learn war (Isa. 2:4).

To this the people could reply amen, for it expressed their thirst for the things of God.

The kingdom of God provided the necessary purchase for the prophets. It was their leverage on the most obstinate situation with which they thought to herald the rise and fall of nations and welcome a permanent order. The kingdom was a reality for their time. It helped them draw nearer the Messiah and arrive finally at judgment and the peace of God. It was a grand conviction that swept history from beginning to end and gave man a broad place to stand. Although it has been tested from time to time, it continues to stand firm.

Questions for Study and Discussion

1. The kingdom of God "was the underlying conviction which gave rise to prophecy in the first place, sustained it under difficult circumstances, became the burden of Jesus' calling, and framed the anticipation for the future." How does this conviction concerning the kingdom of God provide the impetus for the prophetic ministry?

2. What discouraged the prophets? How did their reliance on God's sovereignty see them through times of testing?

3. How does Jesus' emphasis on the kingdom of God help us see the role of prophecy as fulfilled in himself? How do you react to the idea that the kingdom of God "was fleshed out in Jesus"?

4. Do you agree that the church is not identical with the kingdom of God? What difference does it make whether it is or is not?

5. What aspects of the kingdom of God are as yet unrealized?

6. What is the promise of *shalom*? List and discuss any biblical expressions which seem to tie into the expected peace of God.

7. Contrast the durable sovereignty of God and the changing fortunes of men. How does the prophetic message express this realization?

VI

Leverage of Prophecy [2]

The kingdom of God applies pressure to individuals by means of society and its institutions. This sense of corporate identity was important to the prophets' thinking.

Western enlightenment man has lost much of this prophetic perspective. He has fragmented human society, stripping us of our association with others. Laissez-faire economics, granted whatever positive contributions it may have made, further isolated individuals from the group, as has the emphasis on one-on-one competition in athletics and personal salvation in religion. Circumstances have reached the point where what seemed so certain to the prophets appears strange and even suspect to us.

Some years ago a Nigerian returned home after completing graduate work in the United States. His homecoming had been postponed because he had degree requirements to complete, and he was already late for the beginning of the academic term. Nonetheless he spent some time in his own village before taking up his duties at the school where he was to teach. From a Western point of view, his behavior might seem irresponsible, but any other course would have meant disavowing family and tribal ties. His cultural background made it easier for him to appreciate the prophet's perspective than does ours.

This prophetic wedge has sometimes been called *corporate*

personality, for it treats a group of individuals as one. Take the case of Achan's violation of the ban on booty, which resulted in the defeat of Israel before Ai (Josh. 7). Thirty-six men perished in the skirmish, not to mention those injured or the goods abandoned in the flight. Why should these have suffered for the guilt of another? Only as we begin to feel our way into the biblical mindset can we sense the point at issue.

Paul spoke out of the same frame of reference: "If one member suffers, all the members suffer with it; if *one* member is honored, all the members rejoice with it" (1 Cor. 12:26). The idea of corporate personality undergirds our understanding of the church.

The institution of marriage is seriously threatened today. We consider the destruction of a marriage unfortunate for the persons involved, but in a broader sense the weakened institution threatens and undermines society. From a biblical perspective marriage involves more than a license for sex and more than two people. At an Arab wedding hundreds of relatives and friends turn out to march through the streets of the village and join in the festivities. They are part of the proceedings—not outsiders invited in but insiders already implicated. They sense a corporateness which adds stability to a marriage by broadening its base to include the extended family and associates.

One reason prophecy becomes so skewed today is its lack of an axis. It can provide a game for the elite, an excuse for an ego trip, and a put-down for the uninformed because it lacks the social setting assumed by the prophets. We may or may not need to spend more time considering prophecy, but we certainly need to orient it properly.

The Nations

The prophets demonstrated a remarkable interest in the nations around them. Jeremiah admonished Egypt:

> Go up to Gilead and obtain balm,
> O virgin daughter of Egypt!
> In vain have you multiplied remedies;
> There is no healing for you (Jer. 46:11).

The great land to the south sat securely, having escaped the plunder which ravaged many others. However, Egypt's clash with Babylon at Carchemish loomed before the seer, as did the former's inability to right itself from that defeat.

Two prophets, Jonah and Nahum, gave their attention to Nineveh, that great capital of the Assyrian Empire. Jonah's message turned out to be an offer of mercy; Nahum's, a preface to doom. Nahum drew a vivid picture of the rape of the city:

> Plunder the silver!
> Plunder the gold!
> For there is no limit to the treasure—
> Wealth from every kind of desirable object.
> She is emptied! Yes, she is desolate and waste!
> Hearts are melting and knees knocking!
> Also anguish is in the whole body,
> And all their faces are grown pale! (Nah. 2:9–10).

Nineveh's repentance under Jonah's preaching earned the city a century and more of prosperity before the sword would fall.

Obadiah turned his attention to Edom, that nation descending from Esau south of the Dead Sea. The marvels of Petra still rank among the wonders of the world, and it was once thought impregnable in its mountain sanctuary.

> "Though you build high like the eagle,
> Though you set your nest among the stars,
> From there I will bring you down," declares the Lord
>   (Obad. 4).

The higher one climbs, the farther one has to fall. No eagle can nest beyond the Almighty's reach.

When the Israelites searched for a passageway to the promised land, Moses sent messengers to the king of Edom. He described their suffering in Egypt and arrival at Kedesh (on the edge of Edom's territory) and requested, "Please let us pass through your land. We shall not pass through field or through vineyard; we shall not even drink water from a well" (Num. 20:17). But Edom refused, and the Israelites circled the area rather than fight against their *brother*.

This illustrates the prophet's attitude toward nations. In the prophet's view, the nation has a corporate identity which draws upon a legacy dating back to its patriarchal leader. This identity is of course modified by the subsequent behavior of the people. In the briefest of terms,

> Righteousness exalts a nation,
> But sin is a disgrace to *any* people (Prov. 14:34).

As any sage should know and any prophet declare, sin will leave its mark on a society, as will the good that people do.

Once we commit ourselves to one direction or another, the prophet reasoned, we tend to keep pretty much to that course. We deviate, to be sure, but from the original course instead of some other. So the patriarchal figure's wisdom or folly could cast a long shadow over generations to come.

Paul reflected the prophet's way of thinking: "For as in Adam all die, so also in Christ all shall be made alive" (1 Cor. 15:22). Whether Adam or Christ, that first step is a giant one. Of course, there is much more to the text than what is implied by this observation, but its further meaning builds upon the prophetic perspective.

A good start might also deteriorate rapidly. The Almighty promised Solomon that *if* he walked as did his father David the covenant would pertain to him as well (2 Chron. 7:17–18). When Solomon's heart was turned away by pagan wives, God announced that he would tear the kingdom away from him (1

Kings 10:11). This would not happen during Solomon's reign, the Almighty added, for the sake of David, but during that of his son. The impact of Solomon's actions was felt many years after they were committed, which illustrates the mix of good and bad influences on subsequent generations.

Or take the case of a young man raised in a home where his parents "worked at" their faith, with daily prayer, disciplined study of the Scripture, and faithful practice of its teaching. One day the youth decided he had had quite enough of all this "religious stuff" and could manage to live a good life on his own. He drew on all the favorable disposition and discipline bequeathed to him and behaved in a manner superior to many less fortunate persons. He prided himself on having more integrity than those church folk. It was another matter for his son, a generation removed from the training he had received. That lad saw little point in his dad's moral platitudes, choosing instead an indulgent life for himself. This illustrates the delay principle so much a part of the prophet's thinking.

The prophets saw that habitual practices develop in one direction or another, one sin compounded by others or a good act extended by like efforts, until the fruit either rotted or ripened. Ezekiel contrasted the basket of putrid figs with the basket of mellow figs, the one waiting to be cast away and the other rushed home for the evening meal. Nahum's protest fills in the portrait:

Woe to the bloody city, completely full of lies *and* pillage;
Her prey never departs (Nah. 3:1).

In such a city every corner is crowded with evil preying on any so unfortunate as to come that way; sin compounds to invite the judgment of God.

From the prophetic perspective, life is a classroom. Good behavior generates good experience unless we begin to take things for granted; then our downfall comes quickly. When we get caught up in the vicious circle of bad behavior and experience, we can hardly break loose.

I recently read a case study about a girl who married a fellow considerably older than herself after forcing him to choose between her and his mother. Their marriage threatened to capsize from the outset and sailed into still more violent waters. They succeeded in hurting each other, piling injury upon injury, until it seemed that the marriage was shipwrecked. The counselor noted that for the first six sessions with the husband he could do nothing but allow the man to pour out his built-up hatred. In time the couple was helped to achieve a workable relationship, but first they had to realize how seemingly impossible it was to tear loose from a situation they had allowed to go from bad to worse.

The prophets saw people in a social matrix, influenced by and, in turn, influencing others. They sensed the nations to be under the sovereign reign of God and accountable to him. They further judged that righteousness would exalt a nation and sin would bring calamity. They also felt the complexity of life, how delayed impacts intermingled until some dominant trend developed, to bring either blessings or curses upon a people. They saw God at work with persons in their cultural and political setting, a fulcrum to which his power might be applied.

Israel

Israel conformed in large measure to this pattern but deviated from it in some respects. How did the Hebrew people differ from the nations about them? They were, for one thing, chosen by God. The psalmist rejoiced:

> Blessed is the nation whose God is the Lord,
> The people whom He has chosen for His own inheritance (Ps.
> 33:12).

The Israelites had been selected to play the critical role in God's redemptive plan for humankind.

The rabbis often wondered why Israel was picked instead of some other nation. Some were of the opinion that the matter must be left to the inscrutable ways of God. Others saw a particular virtue in Israel which commended it to the Almighty. One rabbi proposed that no one else could likely be convinced to accept so undesirable a calling.

In any case, God chose, and that confidence sustained the Hebrews through many difficult experiences. God must have known what he was doing, their thinking went, even if we cannot fathom it.

The prophets also dwelt on how God cherished Israel. "I have loved you with an everlasting love," reflected the Almighty to those in captivity (Jer. 31:3). He demonstrated that love when he covenanted with the patriarchs, delivered the people from Egypt, sustained them through the wilderness, established them in the land, and raised up the judges. His love is everlasting, as real today as it was during the time of the prophets.

George Matheson could have been writing for the prophets and about Israel when he confessed:

> O Love that wilt not let me go,
> I rest my weary soul in thee;
> I give thee back the life I owe,
> That in thine ocean depths its flow
> May richer, fuller be.

The prophets sensed God's unrelenting love as it constrained a wayward people. Somehow his love seemed even greater in light of their characteristic lack of response.

God likewise corrected Israel:

> My son, do not reject the discipline of the Lord,
> Or loathe His reproof,

> For whom the Lord loves He reproves,
> Even as a father the son in whom he delights (Prov. 3:11–12).

Some chastise for their own sake, to relieve pent-up emotion, to prove their authority, or whatever, but God does so for the sake of those being disciplined. The Almighty will not allow his people to settle for some poor substitute when they might enjoy the rich life.

> Why do you spend money for what is not bread,
> And your wages for what does not satisfy?
> Listen carefully to Me, and eat what is good,
> And delight yourself in abundance (Isa. 55:2).

Turn to better things, if not with God's encouragement, then in response to the sting of his rebuke.

The prophets saw this correction as a means to Israel's role as suffering servant, an idea sharpened in reference to the Messiah. But for the moment we think of the familiar words of Isaiah as they relate to Israel as a people:

> But he was pierced through for our transgressions,
> He was crushed for our iniquities;
> The chastening for our well-being *fell* upon Him,
> And by His scourging we are healed (Isa. 53:5).

Israel experienced the Almighty's chastisement, not only for themselves, but for their children and for the world at large. Israel travailed, in a manner of speaking, in giving birth to the Messiah, but travail is not without compensation. Jesus said, "Whenever a woman is in travail she has sorrow, because her hour has come; but when she gives birth to the child, she remembers the anguish no more, for joy that a child has been born into the world" (John 16:21).

Israel was chosen from among the nations, cherished through the years, and chastised as a father disciplines his children. This was not done for her sake alone, for God promised Abraham that "in you all the families of the earth shall be blessed" (Gen. 12:3).

The prophets meant the nations to take instruction from Israel's example—to reflect on the effects of righteousness and wickedness, to see the resolute determination of God in action and how willing he is to chastise as the need arises, and to learn how exacting and yet patient the Almighty could be. Israel appeared as a finger pointing men toward God.

The Church

The church resembles Israel gone cosmopolitan. "You are a chosen race, a royal priesthood, a holy nation, a people for *God's* own possession, that you may proclaim the excellencies of Him who has called you out of darkness into His marvelous light; for you once were not a people, but now you are the people of God" (1 Pet. 2:9–10). While the church lacked Israel's common cultural heritage, it is no less a people for its great diversity.

The church consists of persons with characteristically different ways of thinking, feeling, and acting. Israel made room for proselytes, but the ideal was to enculturate them, to minimize their differences as quickly and thoroughly as possible. God-fearers, or halfway converts, were tolerated as less than ideal. The church, however, is free from such parochial pressure. It can and should cherish the rich diversity brought to it by its many tributaries.

This all relates to what has traditionally been thought of as the universality of the church and bears as well on its unity. "Elect from every nation, yet one o'er all the earth, affirmed Samuel Stone in the hymn, "The Church's One Foundation." The church should be universal in its scope, not just a Western faith or an Eastern one, not only for those in the northern hemisphere or for their counterparts to the south. No one need take his or her faith to anyone else as if the other could not discover an appropriate faith in his or her own setting.

Unity also becomes an option, for unity implies difference-in-harmony. Conformity rules out any expression of creative diversity; unity thrives on it. The church is one, but it is not uniform.

The church has likewise been described as *apostolic*, which means that its members adhere to the faith preached by the apostles and do so within the fellowship of those of like faith. The first Christians "were continually devoting themselves to the apostles' teaching and to fellowship" (Acts 2:42), as should others professing that name.

Christians must be able to recite the Apostles' Creed in any language and take the Lord's Supper with persons from any regional background. This is what Samuel Stone called "mystic sweet communion." The church presents a united front, one faith and one family. It also passes for a "holy nation" set aside to serve God, analogous to the Levites who were singled out of the twelve tribes as the family of priests. The church functions as a community in intercession for those around them.

With prayer belongs purity. The priestly people should abstain from even the appearance of evil. They lift holy hands in prayer for their fellows. Their sanctity, universality, unity, and apostolicity are the distinguishing marks of the church. They are "a chosen race," as was Israel before them, whose mission is to further implement God's redemptive concern.

The prophets applied their leverage in corporate settings to the nations, Israel, and the church. They saw man in relationship to others, alienated and in need of reconciliation. They plead that righteousness might prevail and wickedness be turned aside. Israel dramatized the prophet's theme for all the world to see, and the church took that original play on tour.

Questions for Study and Discussion

1. Do you agree that prophecy may "provide a game for the elite, an excuse for an ego trip, and a putdown for the uninformed because it lacks the social setting assumed by the prophets"? Can you give examples of the prophetic theme being derailed in the preceding fashion? If so, how could this have been avoided?

2. Why is it especially difficult for the contemporary American to appreciate the idea of corporate personality? How does an understanding of the prophetic message depend on an awareness of this concept?

3. Can one consider God's interest in Israel a testimony to his concern for all mankind? Weigh specifically the revelation of the Almighty's compassion, correction, and compensation of Israel.

4. How does the church resemble and yet differ from Israel? Trace the concept of corporate personality from one to the other.

5. Distinguish between *unity* and *uniformity*. How does this distinction apply to the prophetic legacy? to the church?

VII

Literature of Prophecy

We have viewed prophecy from a number of perspectives. We have looked at its nature, the context in which it appears, and its purchase on life. We may also consider prophecy as a literary genre, especially as it contrasts to Wisdom and Apocalyptic literature. The one considered against the background of the other two will sharpen the prophetic portrait.

We should expect some blurring of the types. For example, Daniel describes a man "dressed in linen, whose waist was girded with *a belt of* pure gold of Uphaz. His body also was like beryl, his face had the appearance of lightning, his eyes were like flaming torches, his arms and feet like the gleam of polished bronze, and the sound of his words like the sound of a tumult" (Dan. 10:5-6). The larger setting depicted here establishes prophetic credentials but the mode is apocalypse. We should not worry if the distinctions fray a bit at the edges; we can benefit from a contrast without maintaining inflexible categories.

Wisdom Literature*

Wisdom literature draws from a common treasury of understanding. It calls attention to what we should already know,

* Wisdom literature touches not only those works often designated as such (Job, Psalms, Proverbs, Ecclesiastes, Song of Solomon) but extensive sections of Jesus' teaching, much of James, as well as many incidental passages elsewhere in the Bible.

although the application may not at first be evident. For instance, when we read

> Better is a dish of vegetables where love is,
> Than a fattened ox and hatred with it (Prov. 15:17).

the words jog our memories. It is far better to partake of lean fare accompanied by love than tempting roast served with hatred.

The writer continued his comments in a disjointed fashion:

> A hot-tempered man stirs up strife,
> But the slow to anger pacifies contention (Prov. 15:18).

That certainly makes sense, or so we conclude in our more objective moments when not provoked too severely or trying to get even. "Keep cool" or "cool it" we say, echoing the ancient wisdom.

When the sage refers to God, he uses the same "down-home" way of speaking.

> The Lord is far from the wicked,
> But He hears the prayer of the righteous (Prov. 15:29).

This is real "cracker-barrel" commentary—no sophistication, little refinement, just pointing out things as they appear.

Just as the artisan forges his sword or weaves a rug, so the sage tells us how to live life with finesse. He corrects those of us who blunder along, from one day to the next, saying the wrong thing, doing the wrong thing, wishing we could do better.

I recall what seemed to me an odd couple. The wife was one of the most genuinely attractive persons I had ever seen; her personality was as lovely as her physical appearance. The husband was a nice enough person but without any of her superlative qualities. Why, I thought to myself, did she ever marry *him*? As I got to know the two better, I came to appreciate how adept the man was in relating to his wife. He seemed to anticipate her every need, to awaken in her the finest feminine qualities, to let her know that she was loved and respected. I marveled at the skill he displayed, as if he were a page torn out of the Book of Proverbs.

So Wisdom literature comes across to us. It is earthy, in the good sense of that word, dealing with life as we all experience it and with an artistic flourish most of us lack.

It also sounds less abrasive than the typical prophetic writings. Contrast, for example,

> Pride *goes* before destruction,
> And a haughty spirit before stumbling (Prov. 16:18).

with Ezekiel's attack on the prince of Tyre:

> Because you have made your heart
> Like the heart of God,
> Therefore, behold, I will bring strangers upon you,
> The most ruthless of the nations (Ezek. 28:6–7).

The messages are similar, but the former seems anesthetized in comparison with the latter. The verses from Proverbs speak the truth without making it painful to hear.

You sense the sage alongside you, not standing at an unfeeling distance in harsh judgment, but admonishing as one who has to struggle with the same problems. Paul called Christ "the wisdom of God" (1 Cor. 1:24)—wisdom personified, rolled into one matchless figure, comforting, assuring, even suffering with us.

Wisdom literature takes to common ground. It seldom pits one against another, at least not with any relish. It seems to assume that there is enough good in the worst of us and enough bad in the best of us that none should care to deride anyone else. We might say that Wisdom literature is careful not to throw the first stone.

The wisdom genre appeals to the senses, to what we can see, hear, and even smell. When Jesus warned against anxiety, he called attention to how the lilies of the field grow, without toil or spinning, "yet I say to you that even Solomon in all his glory did not clothe himself like one of these" (Matt. 6:29). I suspect James counted on our experience with the crackling of flames and the stifling smell of smoke as well as fire dancing in the air when he warned, "Behold, how great a forest is set aflame by such a small fire" (James 3:5). Thus he counseled about the danger of letting our tongues spread their evil.

Seldom does Wisdom literature strike us as alien. Some persons are more perceptive than others, better able to express themselves, and more adept at putting things into practice. This is the strength of the Wisdom material, and it is no small contribution.

Apocalyptic Literature*

Apocalyptic literature stands in sharp contrast to Wisdom literature. It sets forth what defies explanation—the obscure, mysterious, transcendent. It is a verbal portrait rather than a logical progression of ideas.

For example, John described seeing a celestial sign: "a woman clothed with the sun, and the moon under her feet, and on her head a crown of twelve stars; and she was with child; and she cried out, being in labor and in pain to give birth" (Rev. 12:1–2). This fits with what we have observed earlier about Israel in travail to bring forth the Messiah, but we make the identification from elsewhere. Even then there are expressions in this passage that are difficult to interpret—"clothed with the sun," having "the moon under her feet," and wearing "on her head a crown of twelve stars." It is an uncertain enterprise at best.

There is also the further danger that we may press the lan-

---

* Apocalyptic literature appears in such diverse settings as Daniel, Matthew 24, and the Revelation. It is related in its literary style to a larger body of extrabiblical Jewish writing.

guage too far or reduce it in the process. We must take care to maintain the transcendent quality in apocalyptic discourse.

I enjoy wandering around an art museum. When I find something that arrests my attention, I pause, perhaps for only a brief moment or perhaps for a more extended time, absorbed by the work. I would not care to express my experience in words since so much can be lost in translation. Apocalypse resembles that dilemma. We see and feel what defies detailed explanation.

The longer we speculate on the particulars of the apocalypse, the more we tend to trivialize its message. We forget its unique qualities—its grandeur and its impact. We make the mysterious appear quite ordinary.

This suggests that we have lost its meaning. Perhaps with the best of intentions, we have made it say something other than it meant to communicate.

While wisdom literature discusses those things near to us, within range of our senses, apocalyptic writings point to what all but escapes us. The Book of Daniel reveals that God's chosen people have been subjected to an alien power and his name suffers accordingly. How shall we compensate for this turn of events? We can draw consolation from Daniel's success, viewing it as a testimony that "there is a God in heaven who reveals mysteries" (Dan. 2:28), that those who trust in him will be delivered (3:28), and that he disposes of monarchs as he wills (5:18–23). The Book of Daniel also looks toward the future when "a stone was cut out without hands, and it struck the statue on its feet of iron and clay, and crushed them" (Dan. 2:34). At some point in the future God will set up a kingdom and put an end to all those which preceded it. We might describe this as an apocalyptic leap from relatively scant evidence to an assured conviction, and it is characteristic of the literature.

The Book of Daniel spells out our responsibility in broad terms, suggesting that we remain faithful to God rather than succumbing to the ploy of men. It also speaks in specific terms, for instance, when it describes Daniel and his associates' decision to keep to a kosher diet.

Perhaps John, living out his last days on Patmos, provides a better example. A solitary figure, John was true to God through every discouragement, persevering to the end. His faith was victorious over circumstances. He is a model for the believer of every generation, not in any specific sense, but as a witness to the resolute determination which must characterize those who cast their lot with the Almighty.

Wisdom and Apocalyptic literature lie at two extremes of our experience, the immanent and transcendent, whether in regard to God's working on our own identity. The former senses God near at hand; the latter views his ways as being higher than ours, as the stars are above the earth. The one details the art of living; the other, its fathomless nature, the awesome reality of standing before one's Maker.

Prophetic Literature*

We have now set the scene for discussing prophetic literature. Prophecy means to forthtell, to declare to another. In order to clarify this definition in practical terms, we will analyze a passage from the Book of Amos.

> Thus says the Lord,
> "For three transgressions of Judah and for four
> I will not revoke its *punishment*,
> Because they rejected the law of the Lord
> And have not kept His statutes;
> Their lies have also lead them astray,
> Those after which their fathers walked" (Amos 2:4).

* Prophetic literature refers primarily to that portion of Scripture beginning in the common order with Isaiah and concluding with Malachi, to which we add other comments attributed to the prophets and the prophetic dimension of such materials as the Psalms.

Having denounced the neighboring nations, Amos returned home to judge Judah and then Israel. He suggested that Judah's transgressions had been deliberate, amounting to a willful violation of the covenant, like the offenses of the fathers before them. The prophet wanted his hearers to recall instances such as when Israel faltered in the wilderness and experienced the whiplash of God.

The prophet's message is pointed:

> Because I know your transgressions are many and your sins are
>   great,
> *You* who distress the righteous *and* accept bribes,
> And turn aside the poor in the gate (Amos 5:12).

We learn the actual state of affairs, what they signify, and what God intended to do about them. There is no question as to what practices the prophet had in mind as deserving God's condemnation. By accepting bribes the people had subverted the law and vexed those who relied on it. They also transgressed when they refused permission to the poor to bring in their cases to be judged at the gate where court was held.

They compounded their guilt with religious hypocrisy; so the Almighty protested:

> I hate, I reject your festivals,
> Nor do I delight in your solemn assemblies.
> Even though you offer up to Me burnt offerings and your grain
>   offerings,
> I will not accept *them*;
> And I will not *even* look at the peace offering of your fatlings.
> Take away from Me the noise of your songs;
> I will not even listen to the sound of your harps (Amos 5:21–
>   23).

Rather than easing the situation, such presumption heaps guilt upon those observing the rituals.

The prophet picked up the positive course of action:

> But let justice roll down like waters
> And righteousness like an ever-flowing stream (Amos 5:24).

In other words, Amos said to replace officials if need be, catch up on the backlog of cases, and adjust the grievances caused by unfair treatment.

Some years ago I heard the complaint of a policeman who had the courage to charge several influential persons with violating the law. The hearing was held over until a certain judge, known to be vulnerable to pressure, dropped the charges. This was a clear case of flaunting the law and would certainly have drawn the prophet's indictment.

Many tolerate injustice as inevitable or excuse it for charitable or religious considerations. "What can you expect?" they ask, as if there were no alternative. "Do not overlook the fact that the magistrate is active in benevolent and religious enterprises," they add, as if that should balance matters out.

The prophet had little inclination to listen to such prattle. The obvious alternative to injustice is justice, and hypocrisy makes the offense that much worse. "Let justice roll like waters" through the corrupt situation "and righteousness like an ever-flowing stream." Watch the obstacles collapse and be flushed before the surge of righteousness. The Almighty will settle for no less.

We see from the preceding illustration how prophetic literature focuses on the relationship between God and man in a given situation. It sharpens the outline of the Almighty. The term *God* is perhaps the most ambiguous of all words. I recall a fellow who was especially fond of using the designation to accent his discussion. It became difficult, if not impossible, to tell when he meant to give one point more significance than another. Quite apart from any impiety involved, he was unable to express himself well and kept falling back on the term *God* in a fruitless fashion.

Then, there was an instructor who liked to talk about God

but told me he did not believe that God existed. For him, the term stood for the confidence that life holds some value, whatever that may mean.

Some people think of God strictly in terms of their conscience and so naturally suppose that his chief concern is to suppress their enjoyment. Others imagine that God should satisfy their wants, even at the expense of causing everyone else distress.

The prophet forces our thinking about the Almighty into proper perspective. Micah incredulously inquired:

> Does the Lord take delight in thousands of rams,
> In ten thousand rivers of oil?
> Shall I present my first-born *for* my rebellious acts,
> The fruit of my body for the sin of my soul? (Mic. 6:7).

How ridiculous to think of serving God in such a manner, but how accurate a description of human folly! What *does* God require, the prophet continued, but to do justice, to love kindness, and to walk humbly with your God?

The prophet's words also point the finger at us, as when Nathan volunteered a story for King David to consider. There were two men in the same city, one rich, the other poor. The rich man had a great many flocks and herds, and the poor man had only one little ewe lamb that had grown up with him and his children. When the rich man extended hospitality to a traveler, instead of providing from his vast wealth, he took the poor man's lamb and prepared it for his company. David was rightfully incensed at such behavior and declared the offender worthy of death, pronouncing a fourfold restitution "because he did this thing and had no compassion" (2 Sam. 12:6). Nathan replied, "You are the man" (2 Sam. 12:7). Suddenly, as if struck by God, David realized how great was his offense in taking Uriah's wife. He was the compassionless rich man in the prophet's account.

We have all had such revelations of ourselves, sometimes for the better, often for the worse. The prophets made this kind of insight possible.

They also suggested how amends could be made for one's transgressions. In David's case, the prophet pointed out what would qualify as an appropriate restitution. Bathsheba had been a youthful bride of Uriah, a man accustomed to the hard realities of warfare. She was the tender consolation in an otherwise demanding and even cruel existence. He watched her mature like a flower opening its petals to the warmth of the sun. He nurtured her; at times he was as much a father to her as a husband. David had apparently suppressed knowledge of these facts, if he was ever aware of them in the first place. Driven by lust, he exercised his authority, and not until Nathan pointed the accusing finger did the king realize the implications of what he had done.

I like to view prophetic literature as truth shedding some of its mystery, never completely disrobing but getting in a position to act more effectively, like a runner removing his warm-up suit. Apocalyptic literature is much more reluctant, cherishing its mystery, while Wisdom literature would be happy to frolic in the nude. Each makes its own peculiar contribution, and the three make an effective team.

Prophetic literature further impresses us either as a welcomed revelation or as an imposition. Part of us delights in it as the counsel of God; the other prefers to hold on to its prejudice. "If I tell you, will you not certainly put me to death?" Jeremiah wanted to know of Zedekiah. "Besides, if I give you advice, you will not listen to me" (Jer. 38:15). The prophet knew the options and surmised which would appeal to the king.

Apocalypse thunders and flashes, and we have difficulty in picking out a few words here and there; the wisdom genre asks if we have seen or noticed one thing or another; prophecy speaks to us, God to man. "Thus says the Lord" runs throughout, whether Isaiah, Jeremiah, or Habakkuk is the spokesman, and we brace ourselves for candid words on practical matters.

Questions for Study and Discussion

1. Give some sayings that are not in the Bible that remind you of Wisdom literature.

2. Do you agree that Wisdom and Apocalyptic literature, respectively, reflect the immanence and transcendence of God? How do these tendencies apply to prophetic literature?

3. The world is still populated by gods of our making. How did the prophets distinguish between true and false gods?

4. Does prophetic literature strike you "as truth shedding some of its mystery"? Contrast it in this connection with Wisdom and Apocalyptic literature.

5. Why should we bear in mind the various types of literary genre in Scripture? May we miss aspects of the biblical teaching otherwise?

VIII

Prediction in Prophecy

I have de-emphasized the element of prediction in prophecy, not because I mean to exclude it, but because I do not wish to accord it undue consideration. Now that we have discussed the nature of prophecy, its context and leverage, and as a literary genre, it seems appropriate to take up prediction.

Adam's Posterity

When the waters had receded from the earth and man could once again stand on firm ground, the Almighty promised never again to bring such thorough devastation, adding,

> While the earth remains,
> Seedtime and harvest,
> And cold and heat,
> And summer and winter,
> And day and night
> Shall not cease (Gen. 8:22).

Pledging to preserve life, he encouraged Noah and his sons to bear children and "fill the earth" with them.

The Almighty confided that he is gracious and that he "will not be angry forever" (Jer. 3:12), implying that his anger toward "faithless Israel" would soon burn out. This assurance ran so deep that persons might presume upon it, and so they invite the prophet's warning. "Let men call on God earnestly that each may turn from his wicked way and from the violence which is in his hands" (Jon. 3:8). Otherwise, expect judgment to fall. God's pledge to preserve life does not carry with it the toleration of sin.

The human race came to the brink in Noah's time, as close as it will ever come to complete destruction. It will cling to planet earth until God decides to roll up time into eternity. So the Almighty promised, and so it will come to pass.

Abraham's Posterity

God promised Abraham: "I will make you a great nation" (Gen. 12:2). This is a theme the prophets enjoyed dwelling upon and might use as the basis for an appropriate admonition, as when the Almighty addressed the people through Isaiah:

> Listen to me, you who pursue righteousness,
> Who seek the Lord:
> Look to the rock from which you were hewn,
> And to the quarry from which you were dug.
> Look to Abraham your father,
> And to Sarah who gave birth to you in pain;
> When *he was* one I called him,
> Then I blessed him and multiplied him (Isa. 51:1–2).

Did the Israelites not become a mighty people? Indeed they did. Remember, Abraham was a solitary figure until the Almighty determined to make of him a great nation.

God also vowed to bless those who blessed this people and curse those that cursed them. This is a perspective the prophets carried even to the nation which acted as God's instrument of justice. While Jeremiah announced that the Almighty was "bringing a nation against you from afar, O house of Israel," he also observed that God "will repay Babylon and all the inhabi-

tants of Chaldea for all their evil that they have done in Zion"
(Jer. 5:15; 51:24).

It seems that God meant to preserve this people as a witness
to his name and as a means of blessing people everywhere.
Therefore the attack on Israel appeared as a challenge to God
as well as an effort to thwart his universal design. The tenacious
persistence of Israel as a people was a reminder of the Almighty's faithfulness.

No matter how far Israel might fall short of the ideal, they
could remember their divine calling and return. In the words of
Scripture: "If I shut up the heavens so that there is no rain, or if
I command the locust to devour the land, or if I send pestilence
among My people, and My people who are called by My name
humble themselves and pray, and seek My face and turn from
their wicked ways, then I will hear from heaven, will forgive
their sin, and will heal their land" (2 Chron. 7:13–14). This
was a prediction that would periodically be fulfilled and was not
to be taken lightly either by the Hebrew beneficiaries or by the
Gentile nations.

We may picture these predictions concerning Adam and his
posterity as merging with the coronation of Messiah. Here the
benefits nurtured in Israel are dispersed to all. It is a grand
climax to prediction, as the psalmist described the intent:

> But as for Me, I have installed My King
> Upon Zion, My holy mountain (Ps. 2:6).

This was followed by the new regent's response:

> I will surely tell of the decree of the Lord:
> He said to Me, "Thou art My Son,
> Today I have begotten Thee.
> Ask of Me, and I will surely give the nations as Thy inheri-
>   tance,
> And the *very* ends of the earth as Thy possession.

> Thou shalt break them with a rod of iron,
> Thou shalt shatter them like earthenware" (Ps. 2:7–9).

The prophets saw the lines of history converging on God's anointed (*Messiah* in the Hebrew, *Christ* in the Greek), the figure for whom David provided the type. Isaiah commented:

> For a child will be born to us, a son will be given to us;
> And the government will rest on His shoulders;
> And His name will be called Wonderful Counselor, Mighty God,
> Eternal Father, Prince of Peace.
> There will be no end to the increase of *His* government or of peace,
> On the throne of David and over his kingdom,
> To establish it and to uphold it with justice and righteousness
> From then on and forevermore.
> The zeal of the Lord of hosts will accomplish this (Isa. 9:6–7).

"In that day the Lord will defend the inhabitants of Jerusalem," Zechariah added, "and the one who is feeble among them in that day will be like David, and the house of David *will be* like God, like the angel of the Lord before them" (Zech. 12:8). These are remarkable promises, and there are many others to be found, touching on the messianic theme.

The Anointed

The fortunes of Israel vacillated from rule to rule and often reversed themselves within one monarch's term of office. The prophets rode this roller coaster in anticipation of a more established and enduring order to come when God would anoint a king to settle inner discord and subject the warring nations.

The extent and legitimacy of this power lies in its having been delegated by the Almighty. "To Him was given dominion" (Dan. 7:14). Daniel expressed the perspective shared by the prophets. We feel dwarfed by the expanse of the universe, mystified by its intricacy, threatened by the brevity of our own lives and the events that intervene, but through the messianic reign we tap into the power behind it all, working on our behalf. We also feel swept along by evil men, caught in their clutches, a pawn in their play, until delivered by the Messiah.

When the Messiah comes, the kingdom will observe no boundaries "that all the peoples, nations and *men of every* language might serve him" (Dan. 7:14). But we must take care not to slip into a universalism foreign to the prophets, and so we return to the introductory psalms. Psalm 2 is a coronation text, but it also extends the idea of two diverse ways found in Psalm 1.

> How blessed is the man who does not walk in the counsel of the
> wicked,
> Nor stand in the path of sinners,
> Nor sit in the seat of scoffers! (Ps. 1:1).

The way of the blessed resembles "a tree firmly planted by streams of water," and the way of the wicked is "like chaff which the wind drives away."

The second psalm begins with the nations planning to over-throw the newly anointed king and ends with the following admonition to them:

> Do homage to the Son, least He become angry, and you perish
> *in* the way,
> For His wrath may soon be kindled.
> How blessed are all who take refuge in Him! (Ps. 2:12).

There is an implied invitation here to those who care to join the company of the blessed, but there is wrath for those continuing in their wicked ways.

Jesus took up this parting of the ways when he referred to the Son of man sitting in his kingdom and separating the sheep from the goats (Matt. 25:31–46). "Come, you who are blessed of My Father [the sheep], inherit the kingdom prepared for you from the foundation of the world" (Matt. 25:34). The goats, by contrast, will be turned aside to Gehena (the Valley of Hinnon which served to dispose of Jerusalem's refuse). Come and inherit the messianic kingdom or be cast away.

As the prophets viewed the matter, the Messiah is Lord of Hinnon as well as Lord of the temple mount. His power will restrain the wicked just as it delights the righteous.

Variations on the Theme

The psalmist further characterized the Messiah as God's Son, a fact not overlooked by New Testament writers (Acts 13:33; Heb. 1:5; 5:5). David had longed to build a house for worship. "See now, I dwell in a house of cedar," he complained to Nathan, "but the ark of God dwells within tent curtains" (2 Sam. 7:2). The next day the Almighty sent word with Nathan that David should leave the project to another, Solomon. "I will be a father to him," God said, "and he will be a son to Me" (2 Sam. 7:14).

The language in this passage prickles with messianic overtones. One catches glimpses of the Messiah as the promise expands beyond the immediate point of reference. This is not an unusual occurrence as far as prophecy is concerned (see Isa. 7–9).

What is implied by characterizing the Messiah as God's son? There is obviously the suggestion of a filial relationship and the exacting of obedience. Jesus told the story of a landowner who rented out his property and attempted to get the payment due him at harvest time (Matt. 21:33–41). When the efforts of his servants failed, the man determined to dispatch his heir, assuming that "they will respect my son." With this reference, Jesus implied the unique relationship he enjoyed with the Father.

He also observed: "I always do the things that are pleasing to Him" (John 8:29). An inviting young African told me how anxious he was to grow old. "Why?" I asked, anticipating the direction his answer would take. "Do you want to age?"

"So that people will listen to what I say," he grinned back at me. His culture, as that of Jesus' time, dictated that youth should obey their elders.

Jesus, as the messianic Son, possessed a unique filial relationship with the Father and exercised perfect obedience, as the prophets would have expected. Therefore, the prophetic thinking continues,

> Do homage to the Son, lest He become angry, and you perish
> *in* the way,
> For His wrath may soon be kindled.
> How blessed are all who take refuge in Him! (Ps. 2:12).

Submit to the Messiah's rule, the prophets advised, whether for fear that his anger will be ignited or in anticipation of the sanctuary he offers.

"And I will pour out on the house of David and on the inhabitants of Jerusalem the Spirit of grace and of supplication, so that they will look on Me whom they have pierced; and they will mourn for Him, as one mourns for an only son, and they will weep bitterly over Him, like the bitter weeping over a firstborn" (Zech. 12:10). Zechariah introduced the idea of the suffering servant, and much later John picked up the refrain: "Behold, He is coming with the clouds, and every eye will see Him, even those who pierced Him; and all the tribes of the earth will mourn over Him" (Rev. 1:7). Isaiah painted the most memorable scene of the Messiah's suffering:

> But He was pierced through for our transgressions,
> He was crushed for our iniquities;
> The chastening for our well-being *fell* upon Him,
> And by His scourging we are healed (Isa. 53:5).

The last line reflects the quality of the Messiah's reign, the healing his earlier agony made possible.

It proved difficult to reconcile the ideas of the suffering and the reigning Messiah. For instance, when Jesus announced that he would suffer and die, Peter took him aside to say, "God forbid *it*, Lord! This shall never happen to You" (Matt. 16:22). Thomas, on the other hand, seems to have resigned himself to the prospect, encouraging the other disciples, "Let us also go, that we may die with Him" (John 11:16), as if that were the end of the matter. Thomas saw only a short road ahead, with an abrupt end, and his was no more balanced a point of view than was Peter's.

Isaiah meant us to understand the reason for Messiah's suffering: "He was pierced through for our transgressions." He was crucified, not for his iniquity, but for ours. The apostles stressed the fact that Jesus is the righteous one. "You disowned the Holy and Righteous One," Peter declared, "and asked for a murderer to be granted to you" (Acts 3:14). The scandal of the cross did not originate with the one upon it but with those who placed him there. The scandal of the cross turned to honor for nineteenth-century hymn-writer John Bowring:

> In the cross of Christ I glory,
> Towering o'er the wrecks of time;
> All the light of sacred story
> Gathers round its head sublime.

Peter rightfully attributed the idea of a suffering Messiah to the prophets before him: "The things which God announced beforehand by the mouth of all the prophets, that His Christ should suffer, He has thus fulfilled" (Acts 3:18). The Anointed would bring in an everlasting kingdom, as the true Son of God, bearing the marks of his hard-fought victory.

Jesus

Jesus was born into this atmosphere of expectation. As it was said of Simeon, there were those "looking for the consolation of

Israel" (Luke 2:25). A rough sketch had been provided, and all were waiting for some figure to fill it in. No specific context for the fulfillment was given by the prophets; prophesy never reads like the event discussed after the fact. It lays out broad ideas and drops interesting detail, but we still have to find how it ties into some subsequent development.

History, in the strictest sense of the term, deals only with past events. Could the messianic theme and its variations be realized in other than the historical events surrounding Jesus' advent? In theory, yes. Even when we have references to a triumphant entry, death with malefactors, and the like? Of course.

Biblical prophecy is more modest in its claims than many who dwell on its predictive powers wish to admit. Those people who use biblical prophecy to set precise dates, make absolute identifications, and describe in great detail the order of events are misinterpreting its intent. We should rather think of history as providing a *fit* for us, a context in which prediction finds its resting place. History itself correlates expectation with event.

The early Christian preachers illustrated how to view fulfillment. For instance, Peter picked up a reference from another coronation psalm:

> The Lord said to my Lord,
> "Sit at My right hand,
> Until I make Thine enemies a footstool for Thy feet" (Acts 2:34–35; see Ps. 110:1).

The apostle concluded: "Therefore let all the house of Israel know for certain that God has made Him both Lord and Christ —this Jesus whom you crucified" (Acts 2:36). The motif of Messiah reigning comes through clearly, as does the variation on the Anointed as suffering.

"Now when they heard *this*, they were pierced to the heart, and said to Peter and the rest of the apostles, 'Brethren, what shall we do?' " (Acts 2:37). Peter prescribed repenting and identifying with the messianic people by baptism, accompanied by forgiveness and the gift of the Holy Spirit.

Stephen turned prophecy around for those bent on silencing him (Acts 7). He traced the long course of Israel's stubborn rejection of the prophets and now of the Messiah. "You also took along the tabernacle of Moloch and the star of the god Rompha, the images which you made to worship them" (Acts 7:43; see Amos 5:26). "Which one of the prophets did your fathers not persecute? And they killed those who had previously announced the coming of the Righteous One, whose betrayers and murderers you have now become; you who received the law as ordained by angels, and *yet* did not keep it" (Acts 7:52–53). They had resisted the prophetic message that originated with Moses and was fulfilled in "that prophet" to come (see Acts 3:22–23).

Here the idea of the two ways reveals itself, not that it was ever far from the prophet's thinking, but one might dwell on the alternative of the righteous or the wicked. Peter had taken the former road in his discourse; Stephen, reluctantly the latter. When stones rained upon him, the zealous disciple cried out, "Lord, do not hold this sin against them!"

Before death claimed him, Stephen had gazed "intently into heaven and saw the glory of God, and Jesus standing at the right hand of God; and he said, 'Behold, I see the heavens opened up and the Son of Man standing at the right hand of God'" (Acts 7:55–56). He saw Jesus holding court as the messianic king. Peter affirmed Stephen's description of the vision in quoting a coronation psalm. If Jesus was reigning, the prophetic reasoning went, then he would soon secure his kingdom and extend its blessings.

> Let the nations be aroused
> And come up to the valley of Jehosaphat,
> For there I will sit to judge
> All the surrounding nations.

> And the Lord roars from Zion
> And utters His voice from Jerusalem,
> And the heavens and the earth tremble.
> But the Lord is a refuge for His people
> And a stronghold to the sons of Israel (Joel 3:12, 16).

It would be but a matter of time before the nations were called to give account of their stewardship. There would be a short respite at most, and then the summons would arrive. Since the Messiah had already assumed the throne, justice would be dispensed quickly.

However, the interim weighed heavily on the disciples, and they retired to the Messiah's administration of the two ways to console themselves. Peter admonished, "The Lord is not slow about His promise, as some count slowness, but is patient toward you, not willing for any to perish but for all to come to repentance" (2 Pet. 3:9). The Almighty means to extend his refuge to as many as possible before he "roars from Zion."

The coronation psalms picture the king assuming the rule before consolidating it. The nations take this occasion to boast their independence and form alliances among themselves. They beat their shields and raise their banners.

For the time being, the newly crowned ruler fields no extensive army to suppress the enemy. He awaits the moment when it will be best to commit the forces to the fray, and then he will take personal command of the legions, "for the Lord Himself will descend from heaven with a shout, with the voice of *the* archangel, and with the trumpet of God" (1 Thess. 4:16). He will stand at the head of his armies and bring all resistance to an end. Compassion and justice will then transect, with sudden finality, and that moment will be all the more striking for having been so long awaited.

Once the legions appear, the prophet's task will have come to an assured end. He will have voiced his last protest against injustice, the final offer of clemency, the concluding promise of consolation. Until such time, he will continue to form a resolute minority, unyielding in the face of the popular but perverse ways of the people. He stands resistant to the justification that "everyone is doing it."

The prophet implies, even when he does not explicitly state, a condition, as when Jonah stood before Nineveh and proclaimed: "Yet forty days and Nineveh will be overthrown." Nineveh was not destroyed because the Almighty is "a gracious and compassionate God, slow to anger and abundant in loving kindness, and One who relents concerning calamity" (Jon. 4:2). As long as the prophets speak, we will see God's beckoning hand, but beware the cessation of their words, for their silence may signal the storm. When the storm breaks, there is no more refuge, only turbulence, destruction, and despair.

There will also be no further need for consolation. The prophets will have wiped away the last tear. The long dark night will give way to the glorious dawn. We will wake to a fresh new day; things that formerly distressed us will be forced aside; prophecy will have rendered its last service.

We look back over our shoulders, for one last lingering moment, to sense how prophecy has converged to this point, how it pointed its unrelenting finger at the Messiah, and how what may have seemed fuzzy and indistinct at one time now appears vividly in focus.

Questions for Study and Discussion

1. Some interpreters equate prophecy and prediction; others exclude the predictive element entirely. Describe the position taken in this chapter.

2. What are the implications of God's pledge to Noah?

3. What is the nature of God's promise to Abraham? What was its significance for Israel? for mankind in general?

4. What is the significance of describing the Messiah as God's Son? What is implied by the designation of a suffering servant? Why were these two ideas difficult for some to harmonize?

5. Jesus fulfilled the qualifications of Messiah as none before or after him. Consider the evidence for making such a claim.

IX

Prediction in Prophecy [2]

We have taken a sweeping approach to prediction, commencing with those promises made to man in general and Israel in particular and drawing them toward the coronation of the Messiah. Now we shall look at some of the sights along the way. In doing so, I shall steer a course between those who expect too much of prediction and those who allow too little. My approach is conservative. It is not calculated to come up with sensational results but to gain proper understanding of the role of prediction in prophecy.

Israel

What is the role of Israel in the latter days? Here we run the risk of the confusion created by Gentiles being grafted into the Hebrew vine. Paul reminds us that we were once "excluded form the commonwealth of Israel, and strangers to the covenants of promise, having no hope and without God in the world. But now in Christ Jesus you who formerly were far off have been brought near by the blood of Christ" (Eph. 2:12–13). God has broken down the partition, which separated Jew and Gentile in the temple complex, so that they might worship together.

Thus, some believe, he signaled the end of his working with natural Israel per se since not all those physically circumcised (natural Israel) are likewise circumcised of heart. "For he is not a Jew who is one outwardly, . . ." these people appreciatively quote the apostle, "but he is a Jew who is one inwardly; and circumcision is which is of the heart, by the Spirit, not by the letter; and his praise is not from men, but from God" (Rom. 2:28–29).

Others hold an alternative position, preferring such verses as "Jerusalem will be trampled underfoot by the Gentiles until the times of the Gentiles be fulfilled" (Luke 21:24). They understand this to mean that natural Israel has been sidetracked until a time in the future when it will come back onto the main line. They further take Ezekiel's valley of dry bones as a more detailed description of Israel's returning in unbelief and being restored thereafter, which lays the foundation for the exhortation: "Now learn the parable from the fig tree: when its branch has already become tender, and puts forth its leaves, you know that summer is near" (Matt. 24:32). The return of natural Israel is equated with the sprouting of the fig tree.

The debate between the two positions generally comes back to Romans 1–4, which appears less than conclusive, inasmuch as one seems to leave that point with the same view he brought to it. Adding up all the evidence only creates a stand-off, and one's position is determined more often than not by one's preconceived notions.

Israel figures prominently in prediction, but whether it is the natural Israel or the church that is being referred to remains a hotly contested issue. In the face of two such well-reasoned positions, it seems presumptuous to assert that one knows which is correct. When asked, as I often am, whether I think the return of the people of Israel has some prophetic significance, I say "probably so." This answer satisfies neither group but reflects the difficulty of the question as I sense it.

Assorted Nations

The nature of the issue made over Israel should come into sharper focus when we look at the prediction concerning some other peoples of antiquity. For example, the generations of Esau who dwelled in Edom were so important a consideration in the Pentateuch that an entire chapter of the Bible traces their lineage (Gen. 36). This subject is taken up as well by the prophets, including Isaiah, Jeremiah, Ezekiel, Joel, Amos, and Obadiah, to name only a few.

Edom is described as the *brother* of Israel. Esau was promised prosperity and the prospect of breaking the hold of Israel (Gen. 27:39–40). The latter pledge was kept, with Edom establishing a kingdom of her own (2 Kings 8:20). But what happens if we press the prediction further? I recall discussing this question with a Palestinian Arab who protested against Zionism because it was a repudiation of the promise given to Esau. It was not the slant I have become accustomed to hearing, but it was not necessarily false for that reason. It must be noted, however, that Obadiah painted a dismal portrait of Edom's future.

> Then the house of Jacob will be a fire
> And the house of Joseph a flame;
> But the house of Israel *will be* as stubble (Obad. 18).

No doubt this marked the demise of Edom as a political entity. "Then *those of* the Negev," the prophet volunteered, "will possess the mountain of Esau" (Obad. 19).

The issue, as pressed by this Arab, was whether the promise extended to Edom through Esau applies in some continuing way today. It is a captivating question but one I am not prepared to answer.

Babylon provides a clearer case in point. Jeremiah was directed to inscribe the calamities to befall Babylon in a book, tie a stone to it, and throw the book into the middle of the Euphrates. "Just so shall Babylon sink down and not rise again," the prophet was to declare, "because of the calamity that I am going to bring upon her; and they will become exhausted" (Jer. 51:64). It was a pointed prediction which was subsequently realized. No ambiguity was intended by the message, and none resulted.

Much later John heralded Babylon's destruction as though history were to repeat itself. "Fallen, fallen is Babylon the great! And she has become a dwelling place of demons and a prison of every unclean spirit, and a prison of every unclean and hateful bird. For all the nations have drunk of the wine of the passion of her immorality, and the kings of the earth have committed *acts of* immorality with her, and the merchants of the earth have become rich by the wealth of her sensuality" (Rev. 18:2–3). Here Babylon is portrayed as the symbol of all forces that resist the Almighty, mock his people, and prosper from their evil ways.

Commentaries on the above passage from Revelation submit that John's reference to Babylon is a veiled allusion to Rome. From the shore of Patmos, where the apostle had been exiled for his faith, Rome took on the oppressive character of Babylon before it.

Fewer persons will carry the logic of this transition a step further. They still assume that we *must* have a revival of the Roman Empire or a coalition to which Rome is a party to satisfy the condition of the prophecy. I doubt that this is the case. I see no compelling reason Rome must be the final Babylon, any more than Babylon must play its own role. Another candidate, perhaps yet to rise among the nations, could assume that unenvious part.

In another instance, Magog shows up in prophecy to gather forces for a final challenge to Christ's reign (Rev. 20:8; see

Ezek. 38–39). John picked up Ezekiel's earlier reference, probably elicited by the Scythian incursions, those seemingly endless hordes of warriors from distant regions to the north. But should we tie Magog to modern Russia? Not necessarily.

National identity begins to lose its significance as the thing it symbolizes gains acceptance. What Magog signified, the massive buildup of remote peoples and the utter devastation they threaten, will live on in prophecy when the Scythians (and perhaps the Russians as well) have ceased to be.

Israel seems to have persisted as a people, almost to the embarrassment of certain Christians who feel that Israel should now retire since the church has become the people of God. Here we have a people of antiquity outliving the character it sponsored. If it is not a unique situation, it is certainly an exceptional one.

So the prophets predict the future of certain nations, sometimes in such pointed fashion as they did the destruction of Edom, in order to elevate the thing that these nations have come to symbolize, to fashion a shoe that will fit another occasion at some future time. This leads us to take prediction seriously but to expect somewhat less assured results.

Parousia

Paul pronounced a benediction upon his readers: "Now may the God of peace Himself sanctify you entirely; . . . without blame at the coming [parousia] of our Lord Jesus Christ" (1 Thess. 5:23). Those who witnessed the Lord's ascension were told that "this Jesus, who has been taken up from you into heaven, will come in just the same way as you have watched Him go into heaven" (Acts 1:11). From the latter prediction we learn that the parousia will be a *personal* event. "This Jesus," known from extended contacts over several years, would come again.

The promise of the parousia has been variously twisted to accommodate first one individual and then another; the simple fact is that it will involve the personal return of Jesus. The suffering Messiah, now reigning, is to return "so that they will look on Me whom they have pierced" (Zech. 12:10).

The parousia will also be *observable*. Jesus will come "in just the same way as you have watched Him go into heaven." If they say to us, "Behold, he is in the wilderness," do not go to greet him, or, "Behold, he is in the inner rooms," do not accept their word. "For just as the lightning comes from the east, and flashes even to the west, so shall the coming of the Son of Man be" (Matt. 24:27).

We seem plagued with messianic pretenders today. We observe clandestine figures beckoning us from the shadows to join their following. Their claims are clearly in conflict with Jesus' description of the parousia.

We are also tormented by those who persist in setting a time for the parousia. Jesus explicitly declared, "But of that day and hour no one knows, not even the angels of heaven, nor the Son, but the Father alone" (Matt. 24:36). We should not even presume this to be the generation to witness his coming although it may be.

I have become increasingly cautious with persons whose prophecies begin with the disclaimer, "We do not mean to dress in white robes and sit on a hill top, but . . ." one can be pretty well assured that their *but* introduces some attempt to circumvent the prohibition concerning speculation about the time of the parousia. We are better off letting our curiosity ride and attending to more profitable considerations.

The Lord's coming will be "just like the days of Noah. For as in those days which were before the flood they were eating and drinking, they were marrying and giving in marriage, until the day that Noah entered the ark" (Matt. 24:37–38). Business will be as usual, there will be no clue to prime us; like a thief in the night, the parousia shall be upon us. "Therefore be on the alert," Jesus advised, "for you do not know which day your Lord is coming."

We are also told that the coming will be with the demonstration of power. There will be a tremendous show of force—no quiet manger scene, a ministry restricted to a select few, or a solitary death at Calvary, but the King in his glory. "The armies which are in heaven, clothed in fine linen, white *and* clean, were following Him on white horses. And from His mouth comes a sharp sword, so that with it He may smite the nations; and He will rule them with a rod of iron; and He treads the wine press of the fierce wrath of God, the Almighty. And on His robe and on His thigh He has a name written, 'King of Kings, and Lord of Lords' " (Rev. 19:14–16). It makes one feel like bursting into the triumphant words of Handel's *Messiah*.

The parousia will break like the flash of lightning, without the slightest warning and with colossal force as do those unpredictable storms over the Sea of Galilee. All this will occur at the time appointed by God but unknown to man.

Tribulation

Tribulation is no stranger to the Christian. "Behold, I send you out as lambs in the midst of wolves" (Luke 10:3), Jesus had warned. "If they persecuted Me," he further observed, "they will also persecute you" (John 15:20). We would be hard put to think of any time in which Christians were not suffering for their faith.

However, we have something more specific in mind. Jesus announced: "There will be a great tribulation, such as has not occurred since the beginning of the world until now, nor ever shall. And unless those days had been cut short, no life would have been saved; but for the sake of the elect those days shall be cut short" (Matt. 24:21–22). "But immediately after the tribulation of those days," the Lord continued, there will be signs in the heaven and the coming of the Son of man (see Matt. 24:29).

This may suggest some future period of unparalleled tribulation, especially when related to the dour impression left with us by the apocalyptic writers generally. I feel less than certain on the matter because Jesus draws a contrast between "these things" and "that day," the destruction of the temple and associated tribulation and the Lord's coming (see Matt. 24:3). "A great tribulation" could refer to the fall of Jerusalem in A.D. 70, and "the tribulation of those days" to the persisting lot of Christians leading up to the parousia.

This much is sure: Tribulation marks this age and reminds us of the Christ to come (Matt. 24:33). Tribulation, to press Jesus' analogy, is as though he were knocking at the door. The louder the rap, the more persistent our hope. The words speak for themselves: "But when these things begin to take place, straighten up and lift up your heads, because your redemption is drawing near" (Luke 21:28).

Whether or not we go through "a great tribulation" may be less important than whether or not we expect tribulation in the Christian life. Jesus stated that we should indeed expect it as did Paul: "We also exult in our tribulations; knowing that tribulation brings about perseverance; and perseverance, proven character; and proven character, hope; and hope does not disappoint" (Rom. 5:3–5). We advance from tribulation to the blessed hope, bridging the two themes Jesus set forth in his discourse, and here we walk on firm footing.

Millennium

I shiver to think how many pages have been written and how many hours spent discussing the millennium. John described it succinctly as a thousand-year reign of Christ, after which the

satanic forces will make a last unsuccessful effort to defeat him
(Rev. 20:1–10).

Of the three traditional views, I suppose the postmillennial is
the most difficult to harmonize with Scripture. It holds that the
triumph of the gospel will produce a reign of peace and usher in
the parousia. This view suits the mood of unrestrained optimism
of the nineteenth century more naturally than the sober realism
of the first.

The remaining positions place the parousia before the millennium, whatever the latter may signify (a definite interval for
the premillennial, a figurative expression for the amillennial).
Both preserve Jesus' contrast between the nature of "these
days" and "that day," between adversity and deliverance.

I personally take the premillennial option. It seems to be the
more obvious implication, and it also extends the earthy flavor
we find in the prophets, as Isaiah illustrated:

> Then the eyes of the blind will be opened,
> And the ears of the deaf will be unstopped.
> Then the lame will leap like a deer,
> And the tongue of the dumb will shout for joy.
> For waters will break forth in the wilderness
> And streams in the Arabah (Isa. 35:5–6).

Somehow to translate all this terrestrial imagery into the eternal
state seems to do it injustice.

The premillennial view likewise gives the impression of
wrapping up history instead of dropping it like a hot potato.
This portion from the psalter is an example:

> Come, behold the works of the Lord,
> Who has wrought desolations in the earth.
> He makes wars to cease to the end of the earth;
> He breaks the bow and cuts the spear in two;
> He burns the chariots with fire.
> Cease *striving* and know that I am God;

I will be exalted among the nations, I will be exalted in the earth (Ps. 46:8–10).

God's program works out as a capstone to history, the pattern underlying his contacts with the peoples of the world. The premillennial position seems to me the more evident interpretation and more compatible with the drift of prophecy generally. This, however, is not an issue I wish to labor or make the subject of controversy.

In the final analysis we should not claim too much or too little of prediction. Fulfillment provides a *fit* to predictive elements, which suggests that we should not press our understanding. We are better off if we accept the broad brush strokes of prediction and cease to concern ourselves with the details of its pattern.

God has a purpose for man, served through the choice of Israel, consummated with the Messiah. It is a purpose now being realized through the church and beyond as the Almighty steers history to its climax. His intention is documented by prediction and fulfillment, by his promises concerning humanity —Israel in particular—and the Messiah. Some elements of prediction are now satisfied; others are yet to be. There are many encouraging signs, as long as we keep prediction in bounds and do not stretch it to cover our idle curiosity. We can easily forego an extensive knowledge of the future as long as we trust that the Messiah is holding the future in his sure hands.

Questions for Study and Discussion

1. Were you to choose specific predictions to treat, how would they compare with those touched upon in this chapter? Does the biblical teaching on these subjects appear to you as generally more or less certain than represented in this chapter?

2. What are the contrary views of Israel's place in the last days? With which of these do you concur?

3. Why is the prediction concerning Babylon more problematic than that of Edom? Test the thesis that "national identity begins to lose its significance as the thing it symbolizes gains acceptance."

4. How does this shift from national to symbolic identity obscure our vision of the future of Israel? What peculiar features relate here that might not apply to other nations?

5. What conditions will pertain at the time of the parousia? Why should we refuse to set the time of Christ's appearing?

6. What alternatives do you see to understanding the prediction concerning a great tribulation? Which of these do you prefer? Why?

7. What options do we have regarding the millennium? How critical a doctrinal issue do you consider it? Why?

8. Do you agree that "we can easily forego an extensive knowledge of the future as long as we trust that the Messiah is holding the future in his sure hands"?

X

Appeal of Prophecy

Our treatment of prediction has not been extensive, but it has been relatively balanced by discussions about the nature of prophecy—its context, leverage, and literature. We turn next to the appeal of prophecy and in particular to the matter of morality. Speaking of the cataclysmic conclusion of the world, Peter asked: "Since all these things are to be destroyed in this way, what sort of people ought you to be in holy conduct and godliness, looking for and hastening the coming of the day of God?" (2 Pet. 3:11–12). This is clearly a religious setting, dealing with "the coming day of God," but there is also an ethical emphasis on "holy conduct and goodness."

"What sort of people ought you to be?" Sometimes the issue is raised in the form of a question, other times as a statement of our responsibility or a warning for our failure to cope with it. But the concern is always for our behavior. We permit Micah to speak on behalf of the prophets:

> Woe to those who scheme iniquity,
> Who work out evil on their beds!
> When morning comes, they do it,
> For it is in the power of their hands (Mic. 2:1).

May trouble visit those who lie awake at night to plan evil and carry it through the next day. When "they covet fields and then seize them" or "houses and take them away," may calamity plague them.

We will be better able to appreciate the prophet's approach to morality if we contrast it with two other possibilities. A simplified discussion of ethics, keeping it subordinate to our primary interest in prophecy per se, will certainly contribute to our understanding.

The Other Alternatives

We begin with the version of situation ethics found in the Book of Judges. "In those days there was no king in Israel; everyone did what was right in his own eyes" (Judg. 21:25). This lament over the lack of an established authority and the resulting license (implied or stated) marks the latter portion of the Book (Judg. 17:6; 18:1; 19:1).

The author documented the grief of Israel with the story of a Levite and his concubine who were traveling as evening came upon them. They chose to press on to Gibeah, a Hebrew village, rather than chance the hospitality of a cluster of Jebusite homes. Instead of being welcomed, as they expected, no one opened a door to them. Finally, an elderly man making his way home from a long day in the field took them in for the night. He was not, the writer took care to point out, a Benjamite as the others but was from the hill country of Ephraim (the district from which the Levite had come).

What might have been a pleasant ending to a trying day turned into a nightmare. The village rabble interrupted their festivities with demands that the traveler submit to their sexual assaults. His host offered his own daughter and his guest's concubine to them in order to preserve some semblance of the sacred nature of hospitality. The ruffians eventually settled for the concubine and raped and abused her all during the night.

She made her way back to the house in the morning, collapsing on the threshold, where the Levite discovered her. This incident led, through successive events, to retaliation by the other tribes of Israel and the near annihilation of Benjamin (see Judg. 19).

"Everyone did what was right in his own eyes"—the Levite in misjudging the safety of Gibeah; the host in offerring the man's concubine to the rabble; the tribes in taking vengeance. Each compounded the evil done by the other, with chaos the result. Not one of them was able to rise above the situation which pulled him under.

Situation ethics posits that the context can generate its own definition of love and responsibility. From the prophetic point of view it assumes far too much. The situation can produce some semblance of morality, but there is no more reason to expect that this "relative" morality will succeed any better than it did back in those dismal days of the judges.

If we claim love as our sole guide in making ethical decisions, the prophets want to know "whose love, as illustrated by what behavior?"

The prophet presented the context in which he understood the term: "When Israel *was* a youth I loved him, and out of Egypt I called My son" (Hos. 11:1). Now love has a point of reference, God, and some description, resembling the deliverance of Israel from its Egyptian bondage. Otherwise, *love* passes for anything one cares to make out of it.

The prophets were no happier with an unimaginative application of the past than abandonment to the existing situation. God complained about the religious ritual:

> When you come to appear before Me,
> Who requires of you this trampling of My courts? . . .
> I hate your new moon *festivals* and your appointed feasts,
> They have become a burden to Me.
> I am weary of bearing *them* (Isa. 1:12, 14).

They went through the same motions, passed on by tradition, without coming to grips with their current responsibilities.

> Learn to do good;
> Seek justice,
> Reprove the ruthless;
> Defend the orphan,
> Plead for the widow (Isa. 1:17).

God admonished them to be concerned for their present situation in which ruthlessness and exploitation persisted under the guise of meticulous religious observance.

Traditional ethics leans toward an uncreative appeal to tradition and flirts with legalism for that reason. We may think of it as overloading the situation with moralizations, virtually stifling the interplay necessary to reach the right decisions. People who rely on traditional ethics are like people who will never let us get out a full sentence before interrupting. What they have to say is perhaps related to the issue but seldom in any meaningful way.

The traditionalist always seems to know what to do because he seldom considers the case in point. For instance, he condemns stealing but fails to weigh the tension between private property and public domain as developed in a given situation. He has a pocketful of platitudes but precious little that works.

Neither situational nor traditional ethics, as represented here, gets a passing grade from the prophets. The one proves too parochial, the other too inflexible to be practicable. Self-determination (autonomy) and the imposition of others (heteronomy) must be set aside as partial insights at best, detrimental when carried to their logical conclusions.

The Prophetic Option

The prophets advocated a religious ethic, morality growing out of relationship with the Almighty (theonomy).

> Whoever is wise, let him understand these things;
> *Whoever* is discerning, let him know them.
> For the ways of the Lord are right,
> And the righteous will walk in them,
> But transgressors will stumble in them (Hos. 14:9).

Occasionally I run across a person who excuses his lack of interest in religious matters by pointing to his moral life-style. "I do good to others," he volunteers, as if that were all there were at issue. How terribly wide of the mark his aim! Morality, as the prophets viewed it, reflects our compatibility with God.

We must learn to think in terms of a relationship. Situation ethics gets along on its own, and traditional ethics gets by on the legacy of others; the prophet's ethic instructs us to walk with God. When King Jehoshaphat appointed judges over the various districts, he warned, "Let the fear of the Lord be upon you; be very careful what you do, for the Lord our God will have no part in unrighteousness, or partiality, or the taking of a bribe" (2 Chron. 19:7). Do not suppose that you can act unjustly and walk with God. The Almighty shows no partiality, nor will he be in partnership with those who do.

In addition to relationship, the prophet's ethic implied the exercise of justice. Resist "the taking of a bribe"; show no partiality. Injustice originates in succumbing to such temptations.

The prophet was also burdened by his compassion for others and was concerned for the dire situations in which they often found themselves. The Almighty chided Jonah over his displeasure at seeing Nineveh spared: "Do you have good reason to be angry? . . . You had compassion on the plant for which you did not work, and *which* you did not cause to grow, . . . And should I not have compassion on Nineveh, the great city in which there are more than 120,000 persons who do not know *the difference* between their right and left hand, as well as many animals?" (Jon. 4:4, 10–11). How could Jonah show pity for a plant, to whose growth he had contributed nothing, and none for a great city, nurtured by God? He was a disgrace to the prophetic code, a reluctant prophet at first and a lacking prophet in the end.

The disciples showed similar indifference when they inquired of the Lord if they should command fire to come down from heaven to consume a Samaritan village that had denied them hospitality. Their suggestion solicited Jesus' rebuke (Luke 9:54–55).

On another occasion Jesus instructed his disciples on the importance of compassion and told the story of a man accosted as he traveled the Jericho road (Luke 10:30–37). A priest came along and skirted by on the other side of the road, as did a Levite some time later. Then a Samaritan came along, and "when he saw him, he felt compassion." Sizing up the situation, the Samaritan bound up the man's wounds, took him "on his own beast" to an inn, and cared for him there. The next day, he instructed the innkeeper to nurse the man back to health, and he promised to repay the innkeeper for any services not covered by the initial payment. This story tells more about the nature of compassion than all the definitions rolled into one.

Although I have always considered justice an important concern of the prophets, I have not always associated them with the quality of compassion. But they demonstrated both characteristics in equal measure. In fact, we often have difficulty separating them, as illustrated by the Almighty's promise to "be a swift witness against the sorcerers and against the adulterers and against those who swear falsely, and against those who oppress the wage earner in his wages, the widow and the orphan, and those who turn aside the alien, and do not fear Me" (Mal. 3:5). Justice and compassion join in procession with those who choose to walk with God.

The prophets also exhibited concern. They involved themselves in the nitty-gritty problems of life. They were not ivory-tower idealists but social reformers. Malachi was concerned, for instance, about fair wages, social security, child welfare, and the treatment of minorities although we may not have recognized the subjects from the biblical text.

Jesus reflected the prophetic sentiment: "The worker is worthy of his support" (Matt. 10:10). Often the affluent have taken advantage of the desperation of the poor to reduce wages to little more than subsistence level. We could expect the prophet to speak out against such conditions as the company-constructed coal-mining town, set up to provide maximum profit but with little concern for those who must live in it.

The lot of the widow in biblical culture could become desperate unless she was cared for by a son or by the extended family. She might be reduced to begging or prostitution. When the prophet reminded his hearers of the widow's plight, he expressed a concern for social security.

The orphan had little more to look forward to. In many parts of the world today one still sees homeless waifs trying to scratch out something to eat and a roof for the night. The prophets kept this pathetic sight fresh before their audience.

Within Israel, aliens were seldom treated with the same consideration as Hebrews unless there was some prestige attached to them. "Those dogs" deserved nothing better than crumbs from the table, the thinking went. The prophets were also concerned for aliens.

The prophetic morality was religious in nature and expressed itself in relationship to justice, compassion for others, and concern for the issues with which they struggled. It now remains for us to see how Jesus tied the ethic together.

The Resumé

A certain expert in religious law approached Jesus with the question, "Teacher, which is the great commandment in the Law?" (Matt. 22:36). "You shall love the Lord your God with

all your heart, and with all your soul, and with all your mind"
(Matt. 22:37), Jesus replied, identifying this as the foremost
commandment. The second was of compatible nature: "You
shall love your neighbor as yourself." "On these two commandments," the Teacher concluded, "depend the whole Law and the
Prophets" (Matt 22:39–40).

Jesus grounded his ethic, as did the prophets before him, in
an abandoning love of God. The prophets often used the analogy of marriage to convey this idea, comparing the marriage
covenant to a people's covenant with God. So Jerusalem received the threat: "I shall judge you, like women who commit
adultery . . . I shall also give you into the hands of your lovers,
and they will tear down your shrines, demolish your high places,
strip you of your clothing, take away your jewels, and will leave
you naked and bare" (Ezek. 16:38–39).

Thus the heart of God went out to his people:

> You have made my heart beat faster, my sister, *my* bride;
> You have made my heart beat faster with a single *glance* of
>   your eyes,
> With a single strand of your necklace.
> How beautiful is your love, my sister, *my* bride!
> How much better is your love than wine,
> And the fragrance of your oils
> Than all *kinds* of spices! (Song of Sol. 4:9–10).

At least in this instance, love is in the eyes of the beholder.

And the people responded:

> I am my beloved's,
> And his desire is for me.
> Come, my beloved, let us go out into the country,
> Let us spend the night in the villages.
> Let us rise early *and go* to the vineyards;
> Let us see whether the vine has budded
> *And its* blossoms have opened,

And whether the pomegranates have bloomed.
There I will give you my love (Song of Sol. 7:10–12).

The prophets dealt with such imagery as they reflected on the relationship of God to his people, and their ethic grew out of it. Life resembled the chaste commitment of a bride to her husband.

John concluded, "We love, because He first loved us" (1 John 4:19). The prophets conceived of a responsive love. In our sin we could not offer love, so hardened and undeserving had we become. Our efforts turned out to be selfish exploitation until we experienced the love of God.

Over the years a husband and wife often grow to "look alike." I suppose that has to do with picking up the other's mannerisms, voice inflections, interests, and so on. This similarity runs deeper when we think of the prophet's ethic. The bride takes on the character of her husband; the people of God assume the disposition of God (see Lev. 19:2).

John extended his earlier point: "This commandment we have from Him, that the one who loved God should love his brother also" (1 John 4:21). We move from love of God to love of neighbor by accepting ourselves as loved. This is how the ethic operates.

I recall a person who had developed self-hate to a thoroughly destructive degree. He drove others to abuse him and thrived on the antagonism he engendered until one day he was seized by the love of God. Then he saw that he himself was loved and that he was thus also to love others.

Situation ethics resembles loving love. A young girl once confided in me, "I just want to get married!" She had no one particular in mind; she was enamored with the prospect of being in love. The prophetic ideal, to the contrary, stressed the love of *God*, allowing us to love *ourselves* and cultivating in us a love for *others*.

Traditional ethics tends to strip love down to obligation, to follow rules instead of fostering a relationship. The interpersonal theme runs shallow.

Jesus told the story of ten virgins awaiting the arrival of a bridegroom (Matt. 25:1–13). Five were prudent and five foolish. The former carried flasks of oil for their lamps, and the others, supposing their lamps contained enough oil for the interim, carried no reserve. When the shout went up that the bridegroom drew near, the foolish girls asked the wise ones to share the oil since the foolish virgins' lamps were going out. "No, there will not be enough for us and you too," the prudent virgins replied. "Go instead to the dealers and buy some for yourselves." The foolish virgins then went out to buy the oil, but when they returned with their purchase, the wedding feast was underway, and they were refused admittance.

"Be on the alert then," the Teacher warned, "for you do not know the day nor the hour" (Matt. 25:13).

"What sort of people ought you to be in holy conduct and godliness, looking for and hastening the coming of the day of God?" (2 Pet. 3:11–12). We now have an answer to that question. We should abandon ourselves to loving God, accepting ourselves as loved, and reaching out with love to others.

Questions for Study and Discussion

1. How would you describe situation ethics as faulted in the Judges? What makes this position undesirable to the prophets?

2. What is traditional ethics? How did Jesus respond to those holding that viewpoint?

3. Distinguish the prophetic ethic from the previous alternatives. How does Jesus stand within that prophetic tradition?

4. In light of their general approch to ethics, why do the prophets lay such stress on justice? What injustices might especially invite their opposition today?

5. Why is compassion necessary to justice in the prophetic thinking? Illustrate from the biblical narratives.

6. How does our concern for issues round out the prophetic ethic (along with justice and compassion)? What problems might be high on the prophet's list as he views the current scene?

7. Do you agree that we cannot hate ourselves and love God?

8. Think of Jesus as the personal embodiment of the prophetic ethic. In what ways can this view of his life enlarge our understanding of the prophetic option in morality?

XI

Appeal of Prophecy [2]

The prophet's concern went beyond circumspect behavior to energetic ministry. In this light we understand Jesus' story concerning a man who entrusted his possessions to servants and went on an extended journey (Matt. 25:14–30). All but one were able to show a profit. This servant simply protected the sum given him. The master was exceedingly angry with the fellow and ordered the money distributed to the rest and the unprofitable slave driven from his presence. Here the emphasis is on productive activity, service which reaps results.

Some people think they have done well if they have merely preserved their legacy, like a young man who appreciated his godly heritage but did not care to develop the possibilities further. I could easily imagine his reporting, along with the faithless servant alluded to by Jesus, "Master, I knew you to be a hard man, reaping where you did not sow, and gathering where you scattered no *seed*. And I was afraid, and went away and hid your talent in the ground; see, you have what is yours."

The remaining stewards had one thing in common: They employed what had been entrusted to them. The amounts were not identical, and neither were the profits, but they worked with what they had. "Well done, good and faithful slave," each heard his lord's appraisal, "you were faithful with a few things, I will put you in charge of many things; enter into the joy of your master."

Should our interest in prophecy stop short of service, we have truly missed the point. Jesus confided, "We must work the works of Him who sent Me, as long as it is day; night is coming, when no man can work" (John 9:4). "Here am I," Isaiah offered, "Send me!" (Isa. 6:8). Such is the disposition the prophets attempted to cultivate.

We shall consider several aspects of service—spirituality, gifts, ministries, and effects. Paul touched on all these in a brief span in his Corinthian correspondence (1 Cor. 12:1–6).

Spirituality

Whether Paul meant to discuss spiritual gifts or spirituality is uncertain from the text itself and must be decided on the basis of the larger context. Most translations notwithstanding, I think spirituality is the more likely intention (1 Cor. 12:1, 14:37).

The prophets thought of spirituality in religious-social terms. Spirituality cultivated a relationship with God and others; so the apostle reminded his readers that the day of consulting pagan oracles was past. Do not suppose, he carried the line of thought further, that the spirit of God prompts anyone to declare Jesus as accursed but rather that he is Lord. The precise circumstances surrounding the charge that Jesus is accursed have been lost to time, but the confession of Jesus as Lord picks up the prophetic theme of a reigning Messiah. Spirituality, it follows, is a mark of citizenship. Jesus is Lord, and we are his subjects.

No amount of mystical experience will substitute for a life yielded to Christ. I recall a pastor who developed an extravagant place for himself in the purpose of God. More and more he felt called upon to dictate God's will to others, telling his parishioners whom they should marry, what employment to accept, whether to attend school, and the like. At the same time his interest in teaching Scripture was decreasing. He had, I think the charge not too severe, usurped much of the Lord's prerogative, caught up as he was with his own religious ego-trip.

The nature of spirituality and criticism of what passes for it underscore the fact that it results from a relationship. We do not possess spirituality; spirituality influences us. As John H. Sammis wrote,

> When we walk with the Lord
> In the light of His Word
> What a glory He sheds on our way!
> While we do His good will,
> He abides with us still,
> And with all who will trust and obey.

Obedience is the strikingly simple prescription for spirituality. True spirituality is not the privilege of a select few; it is for "all who will trust and obey."

Spirituality may also be thought of as a pilgrimage. The author of Hebrews, having accounted for some great men of faith, concluded that "they desire a better *country*, that is a heavenly one" (Heb. 11:16). "Strangers and exiles," they were pilgrims traveling home, men with a destination.

Their pilgrimage had a profound impact on their lives. Occasionally I have to drive an extended distance; so I cannot dally along the way. I am often met with distractions which, though not in themselves wrong, sometimes present inconveniences and get in the way of the purpose of my trip. Only by keeping my destination in mind can I avoid being sidetracked.

Some people try to generate a peculiarity quite apart from what grows naturally out of obedience to Christ. The person who takes to wearing a long robe as he walks the streets of Chicago, chanting as he goes, head shaved to a glistening pallor, thus proves the ardor of his spirituality, he thinks, but his behavior is meaningless within the prophetic tradition.

Spirituality implies a type of separation. The prophet warned:

> Depart, depart go out from there,
> Touch nothing unclean;
> Go out of the midst of her, purify yourselves,
> You who carry the vessels of the Lord.
> But you will not go out in haste,
> Nor will you go as fugitives;
> For the Lord will go before you,
> And the God of Israel *will be* your rear guard (Isa. 52:11–12).

The prophet bids us to withdraw from alien people, not in fearful flight, but erect and confident, knowing that the Almighty leads the way and guards the withdrawal.

Isaiah's immediate interest was the return from captivity, but he provided the setting for the much-abused idea of separation. Separation is not terrified escape into some protected refuge, isolated from the main flow of life. It is a confident stand for God in the midst of others, as illustrated by Jesus' courageous walk, even at inestimable cost. He plunged into life and came up blood red as a result.

Paul also picked up the prophetic theme in connection with "a heart of flesh" (see Ezek. 11:19). "You are our letter, . . . known and read by all men; being manifested that you are a letter of Christ, cared for by us, written not with ink, but with the Spirit of the living God, not on tablets of stone, but on tablets of human hearts" (2 Cor. 3:2–3). The prophetic message is not a secret document, hidden away in some safe location; it is displayed openly in public. It is in the world, but not of the world.

Who is the model of true spirituality? Not an excessively serene and equally rotund man who comes to mind. He has withdrawn from life so as to maintain a placid disposition and feels neither the hurt about him nor the concern of the Holy Spirit to heal the wounds inflicted on his fellow man. He is isolated but not separated.

Another model does better. He works with men who distain his faith, ridicule him at times, practice indifference as a rule. He extends himself in service to any and all. He is a man of prayer and study, but not a recluse. His spirituality has a religious-social character. His is, I would gather, *true* spirituality.

Gifts

Paul observed that "there are varieties of gifts, but the same Spirit" (1 Cor. 12:4). A gift may be developed but not manufactured. We either have it or we do not, the Spirit "distributing to each one individually just as He wills" (1 Cor. 12:11).

This should lead us to cultivate humility. If we are gifted in one way or another, then it is because it pleased God to make us so. We may be commended for exercising the gift, if others think us worthy, but we should never assume we created our own talents.

The variety of gifts, as Paul illustrated them, extend from the extraordinary (miracles) to ordinary (helps). It would seem that he did not mean to set any narrow definition on them as long as they edify the community. They are spiritual gifts if they contribute to the religious-social ideal of spirituality.

Some will take issue with this conclusion although I doubt that the apostle would. He reasoned that the Spirit gifted the community through individuals to the whole. We should therefore seek "the greater gifts," not so that we will have reason to boast but to better enrich the fellowship.

I recall a certain man who liked to remind his associates of his gift, as though they might not otherwise recognize or fully appreciate it. He also tried to arrange matters so that he could display his alleged talents, often to the point of minimizing the ministries of others. I don't think he did this deliberately, but he probably rationalized his behavior as being appropriate for a good steward of God. There is, I suspect, something of this man's attitude in all of us although we should drive it out as often as we discover it.

We might therefore value an office for its catalytic value because it enables us to identify, foster, and relate the gifts of others. We should not neglect our own gifts, but neither should we prefer them over others.

The apostle expressly stated that "each one is given the manifestation of the Spirit for the common good" (1 Cor. 12:17). There is an egalitarian emphasis here, attested to by the prophet's emphasis on "His people." For instance:

> And the Lord their God will save them in that day
> As the flock of His people;
> For *they are as* the stones of a crown,
> Sparkling in His land (Zech. 9:16).

Each thought is precious in his sight and is therefore to be cherished by others.

> Know that the Lord Himself is God;
> It is He who has made us, and not we ourselves;
> *We are* His people and the sheep of His pasture (Ps. 100:3).

Since we are all the people of God, the loss of any one of us depletes the flock, and the recovery of any one of us is a recovery for us all.

We probably demand too much from some, too little from others, and the community suffers as a result. We may not be taking the implications of being God's people seriously enough. To repeat Paul's words: to "each one is given the manifestation of the Spirit for the common good." The Spirit chooses to endue the widest circle of candidates.

We likely come upon our gifts in a trial-and-error fashion. As we attempt to serve others, it becomes more evident how we can best do so, and we discover the gifts that make it possible. We should develop our gifts in relationship to the community for which they are intended (not as some private legacy). We should take advantage of our opportunities to serve, weigh the results, exercise what seems to be there, and return praise to the Giver of every good gift.

Ministries

"There are varieties of ministries," Paul continued, "and the same Lord" (1 Cor. 12:5). With this in mind, the early church faced a problem over the distribution of relief (Acts 6:1–6). The apostles were already weighed down with responsibilities and therefore chose an additional seven persons to see to this pressing need. This permitted the twelve to fulfill their obligations (regarding prayer, study, and instruction) to the best of their abilities. The result was a division of labor into distinct *ministries*.

There was also a time in Moses' leadership when duties became too much for him (Exod. 18:13–27). "What is this thing that you are doing for the people?" Jethro inquired of him. "Why do you alone sit *as judge* and all the people stand about you from morning until evening" (Exod. 18:14). Obviously, both Moses and the people suffered as a result of such an unwieldly situation. It appeared the wiser course of action to select other judges to handle the minor disputes and reserve Moses' energies for the major controversies—to designate their respective positions and delineate the responsibilities in keeping with them.

Some resent the ideal of fixing obligations, as though it were an imposition which serves no good purpose, but the variation of ministry means that we can adjust the burden of work. We can eliminate overlap and economize on labor.

Some people assume that an office grants certain arbitrary privileges. I once met a military man who tried to convince me that he deserved respect regardless of how he used his position.

He held his rank by an act of Congress, the man argued, not by merit. I still believe that is carrying a technicality too far, and I nod in favor of Nathan's rebuke of King David for abusing his authority.

Ministries thrive in a complex of institutions. The same individual is not only a parent but a citizen of his native land and an employee at his place of business. Each association places certain demands upon him and requires that he set up for himself a set of priorities.

Similarly the prophet thought of ministries as being service oriented. Jesus told the disciples: "You know that the rulers of the Gentiles lord it over them, and *their* great men exercise authority over them. It is not so among you, but whoever wishes to become great among you shall be your servant, and whoever wishes to be first among you shall be your slave; just as the Son of Man did not come to be served, but to serve, and to give His life a ransom for many" (Matt. 20:25–28). This represents a complete reversal, according to the prophetic perspective, from tyrant to servant and provides the setting of Paul's demand for harmony within the Corinthian fellowship. Seeing the chaotic expression of gifts at Corinth, Paul said, "Let all things be done properly and in an orderly manner" (1 Cor. 14:40). To those who viewed prophecy as its own justification, he observed that "the spirits of prophets are subject to prophets; for God is not *a God* of confusion but of peace, as in all the churches of the saints" (1 Cor. 14:32–33). He thereby set ministerial limits within which the gifts might be exercised.

Effects

Paul and Barnabas parted ways over John Mark because he had left them on a previous tour of duty (Acts 15:36–41; see 13:13). Barnabas wanted to take the young man with them, but Paul "kept insisting that they should not take him [the deserter] along" (Acts 15:38). So Mark accompanied Barnabas, and Paul chose Silas for his companion.

Years later during his imprisonment, Paul sent word to Timothy to "pick up Mark and bring him with you, for he is useful to me for service" (2 Tim. 4:11). This is a far different appraisal than his earlier one, suggesting that Mark had proven himself during the interim. Was the change in Mark brought about by Barnabas' encouragement, by Paul's rebuke, or by something or someone else? We do not know, but both men's attack on the issue may be classified as *effects*. They illustrate how we can variously influence others. "There are varieties of effects," Paul concluded, "but the same God who works all things in all *persons*" (1 Cor. 12:6).

The prophets worked the identical weave through their teaching. Hosea expressed the matter as follows:

> Now Jacob fled to the land of Aram,
> And Israel worked for a wife,
> And for a wife he kept *sheep*.
> But by a prophet the Lord brought Israel from Egypt,
> And by a prophet he was kept (Hos. 12:12–13).

As Israel shepherded a flock, so God has watched over his people. From Moses through John the Baptist, the annals of the prophets document his pastoral care.

The recollection of Joseph also helps put the subject into focus. When Joseph's father died, his brothers were afraid he would pay them back for selling him into slavery, but Joseph said, "As for you, you meant evil against me, *but* God meant it for good in order to bring about this present result, to preserve many people alive" (Gen. 50:20). Joseph had been through a ghastly experience, but in the words of Paul, "The same God . . . works all things in all persons" (1 Cor. 12:6). Through various effects God brings about his providential good pleasure.

I see no reason to suppose that Paul meant to list all the gifts,

but even a complete listing would number fewer than the ministries and would be minute compared to the effects. God has a
way of working all things together for good for those who love
him (see Rom. 8:28)—all things, from indelible crisis experiences to incidentals that hardly reach the threshold of con-
sciousness.

In this connection I think of a beloved colleague with whom I
worked for some years. He influenced me in countless ways. No
doubt God operated in my life through this man's willingness to
assume responsibilities without general recognition, by his
openness to suggestion even when not the most graciously
phrased, by the promptness with which he completed assign-
ments, and by his good humor at the end of a trying day.

At the heart of true spirituality is the experience of Jesus as
Lord. Spirituality reflects our citizenship and the pilgrimage we
have begun—a journey toward Christ and back with him into
the world. The spirituality we discover during our pilgrimage
proves to be a fertile ground for a variety of gifts, ministries,
and effects.

So the prophets viewed the matter and issued an invitation to
those not of the house of Israel:

> Also the foreigners who join themselves to the Lord,
> To minister to Him, and to love the name of the Lord,
> To be His servants, every one who keeps from profaning the
> sabbath,
> And holds fast My covenant (Isa. 56:6).

Seeing the need at hand and God's desire to meet that need, we
can, with his aid, perform a wide variety of services; and service
ends on a note of worship:

> Even those I will bring to My holy mountain,
> And make them joyful in My house of prayer.
> Their burnt offerings and their sacrifices will be acceptable on

My altar;
For My house will be called a house of prayer for all the peoples (Isa. 56:7).

Questions for Study and Discussion

1. It has been said that God is more concerned with who we are than what we do. What truth is there to this conclusion?

2. What common misunderstandings accompany the idea of spirituality? Are there observations in the chapter which would help correct these wrong impressions?

3. What in the nature of gifts should encourage humility on our part? Why is a gift, strictly speaking, not, our exclusive possession?

4. Is there any reason to set a priority on gifts? Should some gifts be more coveted than others?

5. "I see no reason to suppose that Paul meant to list all gifts, but even a complete listing would number fewer than the ministries and would be minute compared to the effects." What implications can you draw from this statement, particularly in reference to the service of others?

XII

Psyche of Prophecy

It has been widely held that man is pushed by forces from behind him. This supposition is influenced no doubt by the theory of evolution—the idea that human life has emerged by successive steps from the simple to the more complex, each stage providing the clue to what is to follow.

Psychoanalytic theory results in much the same perspective on life by centering our attention on early factors in our experience as the cause for emotional disorder. One striking case comes to mind. The girl was an exceptionally brilliant and sensitive person but hardly able to manage from day to day. Her therapist began to lay aside successive layers of her past life, to get at what he supposed to be the heart of her problem. Then he brought her back ever so gradually, building a new personality in the process. It was an incredibly labored treatment, but it achieved moderate success by reworking her indistinct past.

Patriotism likewise thrives on the past. It directs our attention to notable figures who esteemed country more than personal ambition. It also bids us read the documents, exploits, and triumphs which attended these national heroes, leaving us with the impression that the key to life's meaning lies in what is behind us. Such a perspective is not without some merit, but it may seriously distort our understanding of events. We may be more pulled than pushed through life. The future reckons substantially in the decisions we reach, how we think about those decisions, and how we feel regarding them.

Expectancy resembles the hands of the future extended back to us, offering some direction and assurance as we try to negotiate our way through life. It is so critical a factor that the girl mentioned earlier may have responded much more readily to a future-oriented therapy.

Prophecy contributes to our future orientation. It gets us looking forward, to where we shall be rather than to where we have come from. It says to us "from this time on."

> Now return to the Lord your God,
> For He is gracious and compassionate,
> Slow to anger, abounding in lovingkindness,
> And relenting of evil (Joel 2:13).

Wipe out the past and start fresh with God. The Almighty majors in new beginnings.

God Our Future

Jeremiah set forth the nature of this expectancy as cultivated by all the prophets:

> Blessed is the man who trusts in the Lord
> And whose trust is the Lord (Jer. 17:7).

The psalmist described this sense of expectancy:

> As the deer pants for the water brooks,
> So my soul pants for Thee, O God.
> My soul thirsts for God, for the living God;
> When shall I come and appear before God? (Ps. 42:1–2).

We anticipate God on the horizon of our future. He accounts for the excitement building within us.

The prophets set our sights on Someone. We talk about

heaven as though it would be a great place even if God were absent. Not necessarily. Heaven would lose its luster without the Almighty, and it might prove worse than that. C. S. Lewis imagined those in hell deciding on heaven as a likely place to enjoy a picnic, but upon arrival they begin to grumble about the accommodations. Apparently their alienation from God was the deciding factor in their state of mind, and it made little difference whether they were in heaven or hell—they were still unhappy.

A friend of mine *retired* to the mission field. After years in the electrical business he saw an opportunity for service abroad. Although his wife had just died, he left behind relatives and friends and a comfortable home to respond to the need. His decision was in keeping with the perspective he has on life.

A less perceptive or committed person might have thought that the advantages of living in America suburbia were his to enjoy as he wanted. Such a person might say to himself, haven't I worked hard all my life and shouldn't I enjoy the fruits of my labor for these remaining years? He does not think about his future in terms of social and religious commitment.

Reality never seems to live up to one's expectations. I recall how excited I would get as a youngster over the prospect of Christmas gifts. The days leading up to the holiday seemed endless as I scrutinized each package that appeared under the tree. However, my enthusiasm built only to wane once the gifts had been opened and I got accustomed to my newest possessions.

Relationships prove more lasting. Interesting new wrinkles are always developing when one associates with others, especially when the "other" is the Almighty. So the prophets rightly lead us to believe.

"As the deer pants for the water brooks," the psalmist mused, "so my soul pants for Thee, O God." I have never appreciated water as much as when I was walking the land familiar to the prophets. The dry heat dehydrates the body so quickly that one craves liquid. It is a thirst such as I have seldom experienced elsewhere. The Holy Land also furnishes some thoroughly delightful springs and streams. The headwaters at Dan burst forth refreshingly, as do the falls at En-gedi, well to the south. In the same manner we anticipate God, the oasis just ahead. When the burning sun beats down upon us, God offers to quench our thirst.

Dynamics of Hope

The psalmist's portrait proves inviting enough, but we want to know something more about how hope functions. What effect does it have on life? What changes does it bring about?

People of Judah were living in captivity. Nebuchadnezzar had taken some of them from Jerusalem into exile in Babylon. They despaired of ever seeing the promised land again and began to blend into the heathen populace, taking on alien ways. The Lord spoke to them through Jeremiah:

> "Restrain your voice from weeping,
> And your eyes from tears;
> For your work shall be rewarded," declares the Lord,
> "And they shall return from the land of the enemy.
> "And there is hope for your future," declares the Lord,
> "And *your* children shall return to their territory" (Jer. 31:16–
> 17).

In other words, Jeremiah said they should not think of the situation as hopeless. Some providential turn of events would open the way for their return to Jerusalem. They should keep hope alive.

Jeremiah encouraged the people to imagine what they saw no means of implementing, as the first step in achieving that goal. We should distinguish here between two kinds of fantasy. For instance, I might suppose I could leap tall buildings with a single bound, as a well-known comic book hero is reported capable of doing, but such a feat is unrealistic. On the other hand, fantasy primes the event itself. A construction engineer is handed a problem which no standard procedure will solve. He fantasies concerning the matter, turning the task first one way and then another, weighing each variable carefully. After prolonged consideration, he hits upon a solution. He can do it after all although there is no precedent to guide him.

A girl turned Christ aside because she had been disappointed so often in trying to alter her life for the better. "Why should I fare differently this time?" she wanted to know. But she was led to fantasy about the invitation extended her, and that anticipation triggered a breakthrough. She was able in reality to experience the joy she fantasied. We are inclined to pursue uncritically the behavior of the past, even when that practice proves ineffective or detrimental. The prophets, on the other hand, incite us to take a fresh look at things.

Times change. Conditions which obtained yesterday no longer hold true today and will be even less pertinent tomorrow. How foolish to act as if every day were the same as the next! How much better it is to anticipate novelty as a providential turn of events.

People also change. I recently came across a fellow I had not seen since my youth. "You used to seem so much larger," he grinned at me, recalling how I had been when we were going to school together. Now that he outweighs me by about thirty pounds it is no wonder I appear smaller than before. Well, we change least in physical terms, and the true measure of a man is internal. It would be unrealistic and irresponsible to continue as if we were going to remain the same.

We may likewise think of God as changing, not in regard to his faithfulness, but in his approach to current problems and with the persons now available for him to work with. I doubt that God indulges in nostalgia, dwelling on the "good old days," while the present ones go to ruin.

The priests and scribes were more the guardians of the past than were the prophets. The latter were sensitive to changing times and their obligation concerning them. They sensed that God never demands more or less of persons than is warranted, and they expected him to tip the scales in favor of those who trust him.

Psychology of Hopelessness

Jeremiah resolutely approached his ministry to Judah, knowing in advance their response: "It's hopeless! For we are going to follow our own plans, and each of us will act according to the stubbornness of his evil heart" (Jer. 18:12). Judah's hopelessness was rooted in their determination to do wrong. Their excuse "we *can* do nothing" disguises that, in fact, "we *will* do nothing."

Some years ago I was discussing religious matters with a man who persisted in doing things he acknowledged as wrong. "God knows I am weak," he asserted, as if that settled the matter. Change, at least for the present, was out of the question. God had taken that into consideration, he supposed, and had given him a postponement if not an indulgence.

It is not uncommon to blame others for one's sin. In Ezekiel's day parents seemed to be an especially good target. They still are today. "You see, my parents never really understood me," someone says, intending to hang on to sin under the first pretext available.

Circumstances also intercept our alleged good intentions. Saul tried to justify his invasion of the priest's office by saying, "Because I saw that the people were scattering from me, and that you did not come within the appointed days, and that the Philistines were assembling . . . I forced myself and offered the burnt offering" (1 Sam. 13:11–12). He really did not want to, but circumstances overcame his reluctance. Right? Most certainly wrong! "You have acted foolishly," Samuel charged, "you have not kept the commandment of the Lord your God" (1 Sam. 13:13).

The prophets sometimes attacked the psychology of hopelessness from another angle. The psalmist inquired:

> Why are you in despair, O my soul?
> And *why* have you become disturbed within me?

He answered his rhetorical question in the manner of the prophets:

> Hope in God, for I shall again praise Him
> *For* the help of His presence (Ps. 42:5).

The psalmist had lost his concentration on God. The trials he had been going through, coupled with the caustic remarks of his associates, had diverted his attention. Despair gained the better of the situation.

In the prophet's view there were only two alternatives: Hope in God or give way entirely to hopelessness. Hopelessness often works as a defense mechanism that allows us to play out our evil hand, a witness to our ill-grounded trust. An acquaintance once told me of a man he knew whose insecurity was bolstered by his wife's love. "What would you do," his friend asked him, "if your wife were to leave you?"

The man could not choke back his tears. "It is too painful even to consider," he exclaimed.

It was, however, very much within the realm of possibility that his wife would leave him. He had taken refuge in the love of this woman and had no guarantee of its continuing. "Why not commit your life to the Lord?" his friend suggested. But he rejected that alternative and with it the prophetic remedy for hopelessness.

The Pledge

Yet this man had more cause for hope than the prophets who went before him. "Now Christ has been raised from the dead, the first fruits of those who are asleep" (1 Cor. 15:20). The resurrection of Christ amounted to a pledge for the entire resurrection harvest to follow.

That reminds me of my first experience with purchasing a home. After nearly a decade in one church parsonage or another, I was unfamiliar with the proceedings. "You will need earnest money," the realtor confided, assuming I knew what she was talking about. Of course, I did not care to divulge my ignorance, and so I played along in our conversation until it became clear what she had in mind. Earnest money, I discovered, is a tangible commitment on the part of the buyer to pay in full, just as the resurrection of Christ declares that God will meet the conditions of *his* pledge.

When Paul stood before Agrippa and proclaimed the resurrection, he added, "For the king knows about these matters, and I speak to him also with confidence, since I am persuaded that none of these things escape his notice; for this has not been done in a corner" (Acts 26:26). The resurrection was a tangible consideration, not a secret event kept from public notice. It was a down payment on what God means to do for others.

"King Agrippa," the apostle continued, "do you believe the Prophets?" (Acts 26:27). In this way he suggested that the prophets had intimated something of this nature would come to pass. Peter quoted David to this effect:

> I was always beholding the Lord in my presence;
> For He is at my right hand, that I may not be shaken.

Therefore my heart was glad and my tongue exulted;
Moreover my flesh also will abide in hope;
Because Thou wilt not abandon my soul to Hades,
Nor allow Thy Holy One to undergo decay.
Thou hast made known to me the ways of life;
Thou wilt make me full of gladness with Thy presence (Acts
  2:25–28; see Ps. 16:8–11).

"Brethren," Peter pursued the subject, "I may confidently say to
you regarding the patriarch David that he both died and was
buried, and his tomb is with us to this day. And so, because he
was a prophet, and knew that God had sworn to him with an
oath to seat *one* of his descendants upon his throne, he looked
ahead and spoke of the resurrection of the Christ, that He was
neither abandoned to Hades, nor did His flesh suffer decay"
(Acts 2:29–31). This event was seen as a vindication of the
prophetic promise, as well as a commitment for the future.

Hope is not in hope, as the cult of positive thinkers would
have it, but hope is in God. We do not affirm life for the sake of
doing so but because of the Almighty's presence with us and
pledge to us.

Martin Buber characterized sin as the refusal to make decisions, and it follows logically that salvation involves making
decisions. We may surrender to the past, allowing it to push us
wherever it will, or we can tack toward a future point. If we
take the former approach, we do so over the protests of the
prophets; if we proceed with the latter, we do so with their
encouragement.

Some people face the advance of years as the drumroll to
death. The prophets thought of it as the trumpet fanfare to the
Messiah's court. The first point of view makes a person stingy
with life; the second cultivates generosity. The one causes us to
grasp and jostle one another; the other lends itself to sharing, in
anticipation of what we may enjoy together. No wonder an
excitement shivers through the prophet's message.

Questions for Study and Discussion

1. What are some factors which keep us looking backward instead of to the future? How may we learn from the past without becoming enslaved by it?

2. The prophetic hope can be described as being in *Someone* rather than *something*. What is the significance of this distinction? What results from failing to recognize the difference?

3. Do you agree that relationships have more abiding value than possessions? Discuss the issue from both a social and a religious point of view.

4. How is the term *fantasy* applied in this chapter in the discussion of hope? What popular use of the term is precluded in the process? How does the idea of fantasy help to reveal the dynamics of hope?

5. In what sense can God be thought of as constant? How may he be considered as changing?

6. What elements contribute to the experience of hopelessness? How do the prophets treat the malady? What is *the* alternative to hopelessness as the prophets view the matter?

7. How does the resurrection of Jesus tie into the character of prophetic hope? Weigh the question in terms of what God has done and as yet means to do.

XIII

Psyche of Prophecy [2]

The prophetic note of consolation is coupled to expectation.

> "Comfort, O comfort My people," says your God.
> "Speak kindly to Jerusalem;
> And call out to her, that her warfare has ended,
> That her iniquity has been removed,
> That she has received of the Lord's hand
> Double for all her sins" (Isa. 40:1–2).

God told Isaiah to console those experiencing the heavy hand of God, to speak gently with them, and to inform Israel that her punishment had run its course.

Jeremiah also illustrated the prophetic theme of adversity and consolation. The Almighty said: "I will first doubly repay their iniquity and their sin, because they have polluted My land; they have filled My inheritance with the carcasses of their detestable idols and with their abominations" (Jer. 16:18). The prophet responded:

> O Lord, my strength and my stronghold,
> And my refuge in the day of distress,
> To Thee the nations will come
> From the ends of the earth and say,
> "Our fathers have inherited nothing but falsehood,
> Futility and things of no profit" (Jer. 16:19).

The Gentiles complained of the futility bequeathed to them, the vanity in serving idols, and the prophet testified of his comfort in trusting the living God. We are reminded of the sentiments expressed in the familiar hymn by Thomas Moore:

> Come, ye disconsolate, wher-e'er ye languish,
> Come to the mercy seat, fervently kneel;
> Here bring your wounded hearts, here tell your anguish:
> Earth has no sorrow that heaven cannot heal.

Death

We find death thoroughly inconvenient. It inevitably arrives in the middle of some enterprise or another. It seems like the great interrupter.

For some, if not all, it also unlooses a flood of fears. The psalmist admitted:

> My heart is in anguish within me,
> And the errors of death have fallen upon me.
> Fear and trembling come upon me;
> And horror has overwhelmed me (Ps. 55:4–5).

He wished for "wings like a dove" so that he could fly away from the approaching specter to lodge in some safe refuge and be at peace.

The prophets viewed death as an enemy. Unlike the Greeks, who imagined that their demise would release them to live as pure spirit, the Hebrews held a much more earthly attitude about existence; so what destroyed their bodies would of necessity be considered an antagonist. Paul stood firmly in the prophetic tradition when he described death as "the last enemy" and spoke of "the sting of death" (1 Cor. 15:26, 56).

One day I was driving with the car window open and my arm resting so as to catch the breeze. A hornet caught in the current stung me deeply. In a couple of minutes I was experiencing distress in both arms and chest. Death looked like this to the prophets—an anguishing stab that cuts to the core.

The bite of death might be eased with the lamentation of loved ones, the reflection on a life well-lived and the prospect of being reunited with one's father. It was a desperate situation to die without grief being expressed on one's behalf. "They will die of deadly diseases, they will not be lamented or buried; they will be as dung on the surface of the ground and come to an end by sword and famine, and their carcasses will become food for the birds of the sky and for the beasts of the earth" (Jer. 16:4).

Herod left instructions that at his death others should be slain to assure that tears would be shed at his passing, even if they were not shed for him. This is a dreadful distortion of the prophetic viewpoint but grows out of it.

Unlike Herod, Abraham could lay down his head as though coming to the end of a fruitful day of labor in God's vineyard. "Abraham breathed his last and died in a ripe old age, an old man and satisfied with *life*; and he was gathered to his people" (Gen. 25:8). He had the contentment of a devout and extended life. The sage concluded that

> He who pursues righteousness and loyalty
> Finds life, righteousness and honor (Prov. 21:21).

It is the person who never discovers life that finds death most difficult. Abraham, having tasted life to its full, seemed ready to put the cup aside. The reference to Abraham's being "gathered to his people" is obviously more than a euphemism for his demise. The psalmist observed that

> Precious in the sight of the Lord
> Is the death of His godly ones (Ps. 116:15).

This is the glad greeting awaiting the saints upon their home-going. These words of the psalmist are perhaps the first expression of the idea of being gathered to one's people, at least as it relates to those whose faith resides in the God of Abraham, Isaac, and Jacob.

In like manner we appreciate the words of the messianic King: "Come, you who are blessed of My Father, inherit the kingdom prepared for you from the foundation of the world" (Matt. 25:34). The accommodations will be ready, as will be the reception, when the veil of death parts to grant us entry. We cannot say how dark the shadow of death may be, but the dawn promises to break bright and clear.

Life

Death may appear more desirable than some trial we face this side of it. Tormented Job cried out:

> So that my soul would choose suffocation,
> Death rather than my pains (Job 7:15).

Given the option, Job preferred death to life. Having lost family, possessions, health, and reputation, Job considered his friends' effort to console him a cruel mockery.

The sage suffered from festering sores which ran together all over his body, from head to foot. They caused an itching so incessant that he scraped himself with a potsherd, further irritating the flesh already screaming in protest. All this was accompanied by a foul stench from the boils.

However, physical pain seldom measures the extent of our suffering. Job wrestled with the loss of loved ones, with charges irresponsibly flung in his direction, and with questions concerning his relationship to the Almighty. It was as if someone were probing beneath his skin, searching for the most vulnerable spot and then twisted the blade with fiendish delight.

Life often makes heavier demands upon us than death itself. Job saw death as the easier and more inviting road. It probably appears this way to most of us, at one time or another; we may see death as a release from the difficulties and pain life often imposes.

"Curse God and die!" Job's wife advised him.

"Shall we indeed accept good from God," he countered, "and not accept adversity?" (Job 2:9–10). Job was convinced that God's consolation is available to us while we live just as it will be with us at death.

Life or death, these were the options open to the sage; and if we accept life, then we must face the prospect of adversity too. We must accept stress as a feature of life. Until I served in the military, I had thought of courage as reckless abandon in the face of danger. An occasional individual for some reason courted death, but he was a threat to all involved. The truly courageous man experiences and can manage fear. He never takes life lightly, whether his own or that of others.

Some people revel in their anguish; they try to gain attention with it and even excuse their responsibilities because of it. This is a thoroughly destructive and self-defeating pastime, far removed from the psalmist's thinking:

> Why are you in despair, O my soul?
> And *why* have you become disturbed within me?
> Hope in God, for I shall again praise Him
> *For* the help of His presence (Ps. 42:5).

The psalmist acknowledged a swelling sense of despair that threatened to drown him in its surge, and he determined to call upon God. Rather than taking delight in the situation, he longed for deliverance.

I recall a woman who saved the pain she had experienced. Her marriage had been a disaster, her ambitions frustrated, and her life generally unrewarding. She would actually cringe and groan whenever she thought of the way life had treated her. She was a tragic figure in need of consolation.

The psalmist knew where to turn for comfort. He did not look to circumstances. Today it may seem as though the world had been presented to us *on* a silver platter which some thief then makes off with during the night. We must trust in God, for those who put their hope in him will not be disappointed.

"For I shall again praise Him," the psalmist anticipated (Ps. 42:5). God cultivates a thankful spirit in us, for blessings past and to come. He teaches us to accent the positive.

Sometimes when asked how I feel, I respond, "In comparison with what?" I do not now enjoy the kind of *excessive* good health I experienced as a youth. A stiffness runs through my shoulder and neck, my knees are a bit tender to movement, even breathing seems more labored. But God consoles me in these circumstances, helping me to accept such limitations with thankfulness for life and the opportunities it affords. Every season of life has its comforts and compensations.

The consolation of God resembles the future washing back into the present. Isaiah mused:

> Indeed, the Lord will comfort Zion;
> He will comfort her waste places.
> And her wilderness He will make like Eden,
> And her desert like the garden of the Lord;
> Joy and gladness will be found in her,
> Thanksgiving and sound of a melody (Isa. 51:3).

Isaiah promised that adversity would finally be eliminated, but for now the almighty will ease our experience with it.

Farewell Discourse

The time had neared for Jesus' departure. What anxiety this must have caused the disciples! "Let not your heart be troubled," Jesus began, "believe in God, believe also in Me" (John 14:1). "Believe in God" corresponds to prophetic consolation;

"believe also in Me" corresponds to the comfort extended through the Son.

The reality of consolation runs much deeper with Jesus than it did with the prophets who were, by way of comparison, whistling into the wind. Jesus spoke with a confidence born within the holy of holies. Philip said, "Lord, show us the Father, and it is enough for us" (John 14:8).

"Have I been so long with you, and *yet* you have not come to know Me, Philip? He who has seen Me has seen the Father," Jesus replied (John 14:9).

In the eighteenth century Charles Wesley caught the heightened note of consolation:

> Come, thou long-expected Jesus,
> Born to set thy people free;
> From our fears and sins release us,
> Let us find our rest in thee.
> Israel's strength and consolation,
> Hope of all the earth thou art;
> Dear desire of every nation,
> Joy of every longing heart.

This solace, long expected as the legacy of the prophets, is now the hope of people everywhere.

The significance of Jesus' consolation seems to have come slowly for the disciples to whom he said, "Look at the birds of the air, that they do not sow, neither do they reap, nor gather into barns, and *yet* your heavenly Father feeds them. Are you not worth much more than they?" (Matt. 6:26). Jesus also cared for those entrusted to him. "While I was with them, I was keeping them in Thy name which Thou hast given Me," Jesus confessed, "and I guarded them, and not one of them perished but the son of perdition" (John 17:12). A theme of consolation ran throughout Jesus' ministry. It could be seen in the manner in which he set the course for discipleship, in the way he assisted the disciples, and in the way he took his leave.

Jesus' final consolation, however, was his promise of the indwelling presence of the Holy Spirit (John 14:16–17). "You know Him because He abides with you, and will be in you" (John 14:17). Jesus anticipated a new relationship between the Holy Spirit and his followers. The Holy Spirit would instruct them more fully and attend their ministry wherever they might go.

There is some substance to the complaint that we live on the right side of Calvary but on the wrong side of Pentecost. Jesus clearly admonished the disciples to expect great things from his intercession and from the Holy Spirit's inhabiting them. It is no small compensation to have the Spirit in residence; we enjoy a God-sized consolation no less than those who experienced the Lord's public ministry.

The presence of the Holy Spirit accounts for the attitude of Stephen as he faced the shower of rocks, the courage of Peter and John before the Sanhedrin, and the complacency of Paul and Silas in the Philippian jail. Words of forgiveness, fearless proclamation, and songs in the night merge as a logical result of being so greatly consoled. The acts of the apostles were the evidence of another Comforter working in their midst. The apostles in turn comforted the afflicted so that those comforted might console others (2 Cor. 1:3–4).

The Constant

God is permanent in the midst of changing circumstances and our unpredictable response to them. In the words of Henry Francis Lyte,

> Swift to its close ebbs out life's little day,
> Earth's joys grow dim, its glories pass away,
> Change and decay in all around I see;
> O thou who changest not, abide with me!

Only the Almighty resists the erosion of time.

The psalmist pressed the theme with a sweep of history and a projection for the future:

> Lord, Thou has been our dwelling place in all generations.
> Before the mountains were born,
> Or Thou didst give birth to the earth and the world,
> Even from everlasting to everlasting, Thou art God (Ps. 90:1–2).

Count the generations backward from our own—our parents, their parents, and so forth—and we shall discover no other habitation. Either we reside in God, or we enjoy no refuge from the elements. Imagine also the generations that may yet be— our children, their children, and so on. As long as time lingers, there will be no alternative accommodation. This contrast of change with constancy runs throughout the prophets.

> Why do you spend money for what is not bread,
> And your wages for what does not satisfy?
> Listen carefully to Me, and eat what is good,
> And delight yourself in abundance (Isa. 55:2).

Why expend ourselves for what proves so fleeting? We are much better off securing the future with "an everlasting covenant."

Change holds no fear for those who can appreciate the constancy of God.

> As for man, his days are like grass;
> As a flower of the field, so he flourishes.
> When the wind has passed over it, it is no more;
> And its place acknowledges it no longer.
> But the lovingkindness of the Lord is from everlasting to everlasting on those who fear Him,
> And His righteousness to children's children,
> To those who keep His covenant,
> And who remember His precepts to do them (Ps. 103:15–17).

The man who fears God can take the remainder of life in stride. The past documents God's faithfulness; the future promises its continuance. He sustains us through the changing fortunes of life. We require no more.

The prophets warned against building on shifting sand rather than on solid rock, or trusting in the chariots of Egypt instead of the living God. Similarly, today we should beware of depending on a nuclear strike force instead of demonstrating our honor with the proclamation "in God we trust."

When picking my way through ancient ruins, I never cease to marvel at the impermanence of civilization. Here rise marvelous columns, meant to support what lies as rubble at their base. They are reminders of what were once massive walls and towers, silent sentinels of a city long since abandoned. The marketplace, once the busy center of life, is deserted except for a few inquisitive visitors. A great arch through which conquering armies once returned to the acclaim of an enthusiastic populace is now out of place.

The Word of God proves more certain than these works of men. We can count on what he says as true, today as yesterday and tomorrow as today. Jesus expressed the prophet's confidence in the Word of God: "For truly I say to you, until heaven and earth pass away, not the smallest letter or stroke shall pass away from the Law, until all is accomplished" (Matt. 5:18).

Prophecy reveals the hidden pillars on which life rests. It lifts the veil that we may see what persists when everything visible to our sight falls into decay. It allows us to see *who* works behind the scenes, *what* he is busily doing, and *how* we may cooperate with him. Prophecy tells it like it really is, not how it may appear at any given moment.

Prophecy describes how to get along in God's world, what hinders or helps our adjustment, and how we need to relate to the Almighty, to one another, and to the tasks before us. Prophecy is one grand prescription for life, written on heaven's stationery, addressed to us. It represents a genuinely exciting prospect, not in some transient sense, but as a permanent lease on life.

Questions for Study and Discussion

1. How is the prophetic perspective on death unique? What factors contribute to our understanding of its nature?

2. What current issues concern the taking of life? How do you see the prophets lining up on such issues?

3. Is it sometimes more difficult to accept the obligations of living than it is to welcome death to our door? Consider the problems related to a commitment to unrestricted living and what counsel we might expect from the prophets.

4. "The consolation of God resembles the future washing back into the present." What does this statement suggest to you? How might it provide comfort to someone going through deep waters?

5. Read Jesus' farewell comments in John 14. How does he seek to fortify the disciples for the days ahead? What abiding consolation do you derive from the passage?